FIT FOR BATTLE

FIT FOR BATTLE

THE CHARACTER, WEAPONS AND STRATEGIES OF THE SPIRITUAL WARRIOR

SAMMY TIPPIT

MOODY PRESS
CHICAGO

To Guy Wolcott,
a real friend in Christ and a proven friend
of Eastern European Christians,

and to the men and women
of Eastern Europe who suffered
as good soldiers of
Jesus Christ under communism,

and the new generation of believers
in the West as well as Eastern Europe,
who face the challenge of reaching
the world for Christ

Contents

Preface

Seize
the Moment

We are living in a unique period of world history. Rapid changes are reshaping nations, and old ideologies are crumbling, leaving an ideological, moral, and spiritual vacuum in the human heart. This may be the greatest opportunity for world evangelization the Christian church has ever known. Will the church rise to the occasion and seize the moment?

A couple of years ago I met with several U.S. congressional leaders and introduced a high ranking member of the newly formed Moldavian Parliament. Parliamentarian Nicolai Kostin told the American leaders, "The West must act quickly and decisively to help us. If changes do not come soon to our country, the people may say that we were better off with communism. And the West will have missed the greatest opportunity to change history this century."

Kostin was speaking about crucial changes in Moldavia, a former republic of the Soviet Union. If Moldavia needs change in the political realm, change is needed even more urgently in the spiritual. The time is right, but the task is not simple. A battle rages for the souls and minds of men and women. The battle trumpets a call to spiritual warfare. It calls the individual believer and the Christian church to agonize, strategize, organize, and finally mobilize to capture individuals, communities, and nations for Christ.

This is a call to action. The church cannot sit passively and watch history in the making. We must be history makers. The time has come for this generation of believers to take seriously the words of the apostle John, "The Son of God appeared for this purpose, that He might destroy the works of the devil" (1 John 3:8b). We must go to the darkest corners of our cities and nations with the light of the gospel of Jesus Christ. We must pray down the glory of God and proclaim the kingdom of God.

Fit for Battle identifies, describes, and instructs the believer in four basic areas of spiritual warfare: (1) the nature of the battle, (2) the character of the soldier, (3) the weapons of the soldier, and (4) the strategy for battle. I humbly submit this work in a spirit of prayer that the Christian church will catch a vision of what God desires to do in this generation. I am convinced that we must have a balanced, biblical view of this raging battle if we are to emerge as victors in this strategic moment of history.

I present this book with a deep sense of urgency. I have seen light burst into dark, far-away Siberian cities where Christianity was unknown. I have witnessed faith erupting in the hearts of thousands of atheists. But I pose the same question of involvement to the church that Kostin posed to political leaders. Will Western Christians rise from their slumber, put on the armor of God, and march into battle? If we do not, our children and grandchildren may face darkness as the world has never known. Awaken! The battle is raging!

Part 1
The Nature of the Battle

If some of our Dominies would move up into the ene-my's territory, forsaking the sweet security of the sanctuary; if they would really strike at the founda-tions of the great Adversary's Fortresses, they would soon adopt a different philosophy, and speak a dif-ferent language, and take hold of different weapons.

F. J. Huegel
That Old Serpent, The Devil

For our struggle is not against flesh and blood, but against the rulers, against the powers, against the world forces of this darkness, against the spiritual forces of wickedness in the heavenly places.

Ephesians 6:12

1

The Battle for the Human Spirit

The whole situation seemed bizarre. Much of the Siberian city of Norilsk had been built by slave labor under Stalin's cruel dictatorship. Many of the buildings, streets, and facilities had been erected and purchased with the blood of Christian martyrs. Our evangelistic team had sat down for a meal in one of the few restaurants in the city, but we were still dazed by what we had watched the past several days.

We knew that a battle had been raging for decades for the hearts and minds of the people in this Arctic city and that the communists had been especially cruel to believers in the region. The persecution was severe, and only a small remnant of Christians had survived. Now they beheld the awesome power and glory of God during these historic days of the collapse of the Soviet Union and a newfound freedom—the freedom to worship the one true God. And, like us, they watched as people from this chilly northern city warmed to a message of spiritual salvation.

With a few score believers and our own team of Americans and Bible college students from Eastern Europe, we had presented the gospel in almost every home in the city and invited the people to come to the local stadium to hear a proclamation of the message of Christ. Thousands came that July afternoon in

1992. And many believed on Jesus and opened their hearts to Him in repentance and faith. It was a great moment in the history of Norilsk for the gospel to be proclaimed publicly in the city's stadium and for so many to respond to the offer of spiritual deliverance.

Now we gathered in the restaurant to celebrate the great victory and to give thanks to God for all that He had done. My wife, Tex, had been witnessing to a university student from Moscow who was in the city interpreting for a businessman from Western Europe. Tex invited both of them to join us for our celebration meal. We were all seated at a long table where our team members sat across from one another. The university student was seated at one end of the table and the businessman at the other end. That's when things seemed so odd.

The student from Moscow told us that her parents were atheists, and she had no interest in nor knowledge of God until some members of Campus Crusade for Christ had come to Moscow and explained to her the gospel. After seventy years of government leaders forbidding the declaration of the Christian message, the masses of Russians now could hear the gospel for the first time. And they were hungry, even starved, for a spiritual and moral foundation in life. The young Russian asked questions with a simplicity and purity of heart.

"I want to believe," she said. "I want to read, to study, to know more. Perhaps if I was born in the West, it would be easier for me to overcome all of my atheistic teachings. But I really do want to know the truth." Her sincerity was moving.

However, the response of the businessman at the other end of the table was an entirely different story. He began to spew out his venom. "Jesus was a homosexual. Christians are intolerant. I've read your materials, and I reject God. If there is a God, and I reject Him, I don't believe that He will reject me when I die."

I sat there amazed at what I was hearing. This man came from Holland, a nation with a rich history of Christianity. The great Reformers had set the fires of revival burning in his country hundreds of years earlier. But a new generation had arisen—

one that was hardened and blinded to the truth its forefathers left behind. In contrast, the Russian student came from a nation that had systematically tried to wipe Christianity off the face of the earth. One of the leaders of the small Baptist church in that city had seen his father killed by the communists. He still does not know what happened to his mother. The last time he saw his home it was being burned to the ground. And now a new generation of Russians has arisen—Russians hungry for the gospel.

THE "CHRISTIAN" WEST

But how did all of this happen? How did we in the "Christian West" move away from such wonderful historical roots of Christianity? And how did such an "Evil Empire," as former president Ronald Reagan called the Soviet Union, become the most fertile soil in the world for the proclamation of the gospel of Christ? How could a businessman with a good knowledge of the Bible and a rich history of Christianity become so blind? And how could a university student who has been brainwashed with scientific atheism and who had no knowledge of the Bible be so open to the gospel of Christ?

This book attempts to answer those questions, not necessarily from a philosophical, sociological, or historical perspective, but rather from the dimension of the spiritual. There exists an intense battle in the heavenly places for this generation. The battleground is the human heart. The soldiers are the saints of God. The weapons of our warfare are mighty, and the victory belongs to God. The Western world has entered into a post-Christian era but does not have to remain there. God has given us everything that we need to win the battle and return this generation to Christ and His values.

However, we must understand the nature of the battle , the character and weapons of the soldier, as well as the strategy of the Bible if we are to capture this generation for Christ. There must arise a sense of urgency in the Christian's heart to lead his family, friends, and colleagues into a personal relationship with

Christ. Yet, we also need a clear understanding of biblical teaching about the raging battle.

In the West, an immense assault on the Bible appears to be underway, as well as an assault on Christian values and lifestyle. The attacks of Satan against Christianity have been blatant and calculated. He has attempted to ravish the strength of the American church in three different areas: the spirit, the mind, and the society.

During the mid-sixties and early seventies a great portion of the baby boomer generation decided to throw out "traditional moral values." The Vietnam War was raging. Some of my schoolmates left for Vietnam, but never came home. Others returned crippled and mangled. But the greatest devastation took place in the *spirit* of an entire generation.

Many of my peers "turned on, tuned in, and dropped out." A counterculture formed quickly. Young people began to experiment with mind expanding drugs and investigated Eastern religions and cults. Darkness moved quickly into restless and empty hearts.

MY PERSONAL ODYSSEY

I am convinced that I too would have adopted a philosophy of atheism had I not become a Christian one month before entering the university. I was fairly typical of my generation. I grew up believing in God and Jesus, but church meant very little to me. I thought that I was a Christian because I lived in America. But my life was empty. The lyrics of a popular song of the times described my condition, "I can't get no satisfaction."

That restless spirit drove me to an immoral lifestyle. When I first attended the university, I had one professor who felt it was his duty to challenge Christian values and propagate atheism. I would have adopted his philosophy (as did many of my friends) if I had not come to Christ. It would have given me an excuse for my immoral behavior.

But in 1965 I had become a Christian. The professor, though, ridiculed Christians often and quoted the Scriptures trying to prove his point. His tactics drove me to the Bible to look for myself. I spent much of my time as a new Christian in the library searching for the truth about his statements and studying the Bible. In every instance I discovered that my professor had misquoted, quoted out of context, or misrepresented what the Bible actually stated. Had I not come to know Christ, I would have been easy prey for the spiritual vultures attempting to devour the carcasses of people who lie dead on the broad path of sin. But because I came to know Christ, my heart began to beat with a passion to reach my contemporaries.

While in college, I visited the French Quarter of New Orleans on weekends. One night in 1968 I told a young couple about my faith. They were stoned on drugs and heavily involved in the occult. They were carrying a small child in their arms. I thought to myself, "What will the next generation look like? What will the attitudes, philosophy, and lifestyle of this child and his contemporaries be like when they are grown?" Well, that generation—one that asked why and found few answers—is upon us. Divorce is rampant. Violence is the order of the day. Sexually transmitted diseases are killing millions. Multiple millions of babies are being aborted. Darkness is quickly covering Western civilization.

And what has been the response of Christians to the times in which we find ourselves? First, the church *has* responded to the need of this generation. Spiritual darkness always produces an immense amount of human suffering. And the church has attempted to minister to the needs of a hurting generation and alleviate some of the suffering. However, I am convinced that our attempts have fallen far too short of turning around the next generation. We have put Band-Aids® on human hurts when spiritual surgery is actually needed.

NEEDED: A SPIRITUAL AWAKENING

God has allowed me to travel for more than twenty years throughout Eastern Europe. I have been there during the darkest times, when there seemed to be little hope of Christians' piercing the darkness. And I have been there when light has burst into the hearts of tens of thousands. As I have traveled in Eastern Europe and other areas of the world, God has deeply impressed upon me the absolute necessity of a mighty, sweeping spiritual awakening that must come to the Christian community in the West. The battle is a spiritual one and will only be won by a mighty spiritual revival.

I have observed the darkest areas of the world being penetrated with the message of God's love and salvation. I have witnessed the gospel entering nations such as Mongolia, where Christianity has never even existed. I have preached in stadiums in remote regions of the former Soviet Union where the gospel has never been publicly proclaimed. I have witnessed the glory of God shining into the hearts of tens of thousands of people who had been taught all of their lives, "There is no God."

What has happened in Eastern Europe cannot be explained in mere political terms such as *glasnost* or *peristroika*. Political leaders like Gorbachev, Yeltsin, or Romania's Illiescu cannot take credit for what has transpired. I am convinced that what happened there can only be defined as a mighty intervention of God in the affairs of human history. For a period of time God has opened the doors for the gospel to penetrate some of the most remote regions of the world. He has revealed Himself to an entire generation in some of the world's darkest areas that didn't know He even existed.

That gives me great hope for the church in the West. As darkness continues to cover much of our society, we can see what God has done in the darkest part of the world. Many ask me, "But how long will all of this freedom in Eastern Europe last?" I really don't know. Things could revert to communism by the time this book is in print. But I do know one thing—God has revealed Himself to millions of Eastern Europeans who had no hope of even hearing about Him. Multitudes have found a personal relationship with God.

Every generation must experience a fresh move of God's Spirit in order for the torch of the gospel to continue to burn brightly. Without our love for God and others being regularly rekindled, our light goes dim and darkness rapidly covers society.

One of the most sobering passages of Scripture can be found in the book of Revelation. The Christian community in Ephesus was complimented for being sound biblically and having endured suffering. But the Holy Spirit said to that group of Christians, "I have this against you, that you have left your first love. Remember therefore from where you have fallen, and repent and do the deeds you did at first" (2:4–5). Then the Holy Spirit makes a shocking statement to this group of Christians. He says, "Or else I am coming to you, and will remove your lampstand out of its place—unless you repent" (verse 5).

Our torch may be passed to Eastern Europeans, Koreans, South Americans, and Africans with Western Europeans and North Americans left in a post-Christian era. The great need of the hour is for repentance and a rapid return to our first love.

Ephesus was located in what is presently the nation of Turkey. And today there are only 1 in 100,000 Turks who claim to be Christians. Evidently God meant what He said. The torch of Christianity did not go out. God simply took the torch and passed it to another group of people. It only takes one generation forsaking their first love to lose the light of the torch of the gospel.

The church in the West faces the same challenge that the Ephesian Christians faced nearly two thousand years ago. Our torch may be passed to Eastern Europeans, Koreans, South Americans, and Africans with Western Europeans and North Americans left in a post-Christian era. The great need of the hour is for repentance and a rapid return to our first love. Darkness is quickly encroaching upon Western civilization. We stand on the threshold of an entire generation without any knowledge of God.

I recently conducted evangelistic meetings near the city of Glasgow, Scotland. It is an area with a rich heritage of Christianity. Some of the world's greatest preachers have come from Scotland. Just five miles from where I conducted the mission are the "Preaching Braes." They are small rolling hills that form a natural amphitheater. The great eighteenth-century British evangelist George Whitefield preached to thousands in the Braes. Nearly one hundred years later the American evangelist D. L. Moody preached in the nearby community. Now I was conducting the meetings close to where Moody spoke.

However, the spiritual climate has drastically changed since the days of Whitefield and Moody. Glasgow's motto used to read, "Let Glasgow flourish by the preaching of Thy Word and the praising of Thy Name." Today it only says, "Let Glasgow flourish." One Christian church in the vicinity has been turned into an Islamic Mosque.

I had the opportunity to speak in a number of the schools about my faith in Christ (which, by the way, would not have even been allowed in the United States). Before I spoke at one school, the teacher asked the students a few questions.

"How many of you read your horoscope in the newspaper on a regular basis?" he asked. Ninety percent of the students lifted their hands.

"How many of you read your Bibles on a regular basis?" came the next question. Only one student lifted his hand.

My heart broke. This area was formerly known as the Bible belt of Britain and much of Europe. But today an entire generation seems to be groping in spiritual darkness. The church must awaken to the gravity of the situation and the necessity of a divine intervention in the affairs of Western civilization.

Such an intervention is possible! We are not as those who are without hope. Not only is Jesus Christ the same yesterday, today, and forever; but He is the same north, east, south, and west. In other words, what God has done in a former time He is quite capable of doing today. And what God has done in Eastern Europe, He is ready to do in Western Europe and North America.

Perhaps no place ever looked as dark as the gulags of Siberia. People feared to even mention the name of God. But in that far Arctic city of Norilsk, light has pierced the darkness and won a victory in hundreds and thousands of empty and defeated lives. After our meetings in Norilsk, several Bible college students from Moldavia stayed in the city to disciple the new believers. Two of them eventually stayed to pastor the scores of new converts. Amazingly, the city has now asked those two students to teach the Bible as part of the curriculum to all of the students in the city.

If God can do that in the darkest part of Siberia, then we can rest assured that He is capable of shattering the spiritual darkness that has engulfed the Western world. The raging battle that we now face is a spiritual one and will only be won by the power of the Holy Spirit. We must understand the words of the Lord to Zerubbabel: "Not by might, nor by power, but by My Spirit says the Lord of hosts" (Zechariah 4:6).

William Gurnall, a seventeenth-century British preacher, wrote one of the finest works on spiritual warfare in 1655. He stated in his introductory remarks, "The subject of the treatise is solemn: A War between the Saint and Satan. . . . It is a spiritual war you shall read of; not a history of what was fought many ages past and is now over, but of a war that now goes on—the tragedy is present with us. And it is not taking place at the fartherest end of the world; it concerns you and everyone who reads of it. The stage on which this war is fought is every man's own soul. There are no neutrals in this war. The whole world is engaged in the quarrel, either for God against Satan, or for Satan against God."[1]

Gurnall's statement stands as true today as it did 340 years ago. The battle continues to rage. The spirit and soul of an entire generation is at risk.

There is no grace which we behold in the character of our Lord which may not be ours in increasing measure as we look to the Spirit to produce it in us.

J. Oswald Sanders
Spiritual Maturity

For whom He foreknew, He also predestined to become conformed to the image of His Son, that He might be the first-born among many brethren.

Romans 8:29

2

The Battle for the
Human Personality

With my head in my hands, I sat in the hotel room weeping. The pain was so deep. So many unanswered questions seemed to stare me in the face. My wife and I had come to Germany to serve the Lord out of a deep sense of love for Him. Now it appeared as though the bottom had fallen out of our lives.

Our son, Dave, had developed a seizure disorder, and the medical prognosis was not good. We were told that Dave would not have proper use of his limbs for the rest of his life. He was placed on medication but had severe reactions to every treatment attempted.

As Tex and I came to grips with our son's health problems, we encountered even greater difficulties. I had always considered our marriage to be a good one. We had never had any major difficulties in adjusting. But Dave's medical problems forced us to get honest with one another. As we began to share the deep hurts of our hearts with each other, I realized how much I, as a husband, had failed Tex. For years Tex would never argue with me because I gave her the impression that she was always wrong and that I was right. My word was always final. Consequently, Tex had been deeply wounded and for years had not shared with me the innermost needs of her life.

I was devastated. I began to see in a new way the extent of my self-centeredness, pride, and impurities. I desired desperately to talk with a friend or a counselor—anyone who would listen. I felt confused and in need of direction. But we were far away from home. So Tex and I asked our church for a few days off to talk things over and try to understand what to do.

We rented a hotel room and spent the time talking and praying. When we finally opened up to one another, we discovered a lot of "debris" in each other's lives—childhood hurts, as well as wounds inflicted on one another throughout our married life. Dave's physical pain was forcing us to wrestle with our own emotional pain.

As we talked, one question plagued me. I believed the Bible and in Jesus as the Christ. I had preached many times that Jesus was sufficient to meet every need of our lives. But now that we were in the greatest crisis of our lives, would Christ alone really be sufficient to meet the needs of Tex and Sammy Tippit? It was this question that drove me to the greatest step of spiritual growth in my Christian life.

Many hours and days of prayer would follow that searching, intense evening in the hotel room. Once the door of my heart was opened to the searchlight of the Holy Spirit, however, God began to open my eyes to two great truths: (1) sin has a devastating effect on the human personality; and (2) Christ is sufficient to forgive, heal, and transform that same personality.

Eventually Tex and I returned to the United States, where God graciously healed our son through medical treatment. A healing process also had begun in our own marriage. Tex and I began to communicate more openly, and she soon knew I considered her opinion to be important and necessary. I began to listen more to her concerns. And God's healing ointment called grace began to remove the emotional scars from our hearts. Today, we look back upon those difficult days with gratitude, for it was in the valley of despondency that we experienced the fullness of the love of God.

However, upon our return home, we discovered a new pattern of thought that had emerged in the American church. Many

Christians no longer spoke of the One who is called "Wonderful Counselor" meeting the deep needs of their hearts. An entire new vocabulary had been adopted from the secular culture surrounding the church. Adultery and immorality were now called "sex addiction." Homosexuality was called "an alternate lifestyle."

It seemed that many Christian radio and television stations, as well as the pulpits of the land, had left biblical teaching and resorted to psychological jargon. The new emphasis elevated concepts such as "self-help," "self-image," and "self-love." Pastors and Christian leaders advertised on radio and television that they also had suffered in the valley of despondency. But the solutions they promoted required the involvement of psychologists, psychiatrists, or therapists. Modern counseling methods and psychological treatments were the only way to deal successfully with "co-dependent" behavior, or to help those who were products of "dysfunctional" families.

THE ALL-SUFFICIENT ONE

All of this Christian "newspeak" took me by surprise. Where was the power of Christ in all these approaches? Eventually I came to one conclusion. To experience revival in our generation, we must renew our vision of Christ as the all-sufficient One. We must see that He alone can meet the deepest needs of the human heart. For too long Christians have said that they believe in the God of Abraham, Isaac, and Jacob, while they continue to live as though the mighty God is not relevant or capable of meeting the needs of modern society. Certainly a friend, pastor, or counselor can be invaluable to a hurting heart. However, the ultimate and clearly stated purpose of such help should always be to lead those who suffer to the sufficiency of Christ.

In order for us to see Christ as the all-sufficient One, we must return to some basic Christian truths that have been embraced by believers of all eras. Those truths must then be applied to our everyday problems.

CHRIST UNITED METHODIST CHURCH
4488 POPLAR AVENUE
MEMPHIS, TENNESSEE 38117

First, we must understand the nature of man and woman. We will never comprehend the sufficiency of Christ to meet our needs until we understand the total depravity of our own hearts. From the time of our first father, Adam, until today, we have been plagued with that deadly disease of the spirit called sin. Sin has brought tragic consequences to the human personality. The psalmist cried out, "Behold, I was brought forth in iniquity, and in sin my mother conceived me" (Psalm 51:5).

By nature, then, we are sinful. And sin has robbed us of the fullness of joy and life that God intended us to experience. A psychological system that insists "I'm OK—you're OK" cannot remove the horrible scar that has been left on the human personality. A better self-image will not change the nature of man. Only the blood of Jesus provides the forgiveness that is needed to heal the innermost hurts of the heart and give us true, lasting worth as people.

It does not matter how good or bad our memories or childhood experiences may be. Each one of us has distorted personality and behavioral patterns, the result of the sin nature within us. As we understand our own nature, we comprehend more fully the incredible love that an absolutely holy God has for us. And it is only in our relationship with Jesus that we are able to comprehend the height, the depth, the breadth, and the width of God's love (Ephesians 3:18–19). It is only in Christ's love that the human personality can be transformed.

Second, we must be totally honest about our particular sins. Jesus was full of truth and grace. If we are to know His sufficiency for our lives, then truth is imperative. Truth and denial cannot live in the same house. The apostle John said, "If we say that we have no sin, we are deceiving ourselves, and the truth is not in us" (1 John 1:8). The reason that many have not known the healing ointment of Christ's grace is because they have not been willing to submit to the surgical procedures of His truth in relation to their lives.

I would never have been able to experience Christ's sufficiency to meet my needs in Germany had I not been willing to become brutally honest with God, my family, and myself. Such honesty is not morbid self-introspection. Rather, it is a quiet submission to the indwelling Holy Spirit. It means granting Him access to every dark corner of our hearts. As He searches our hearts, He does not bring condemnation to us. He exposes the dirt and filth in our lives and then rushes us to the cross for treatment. And, oh, the indescribable cleansing and healing that flow from the cross of Christ!

A HIDING PLACE

As we turn away from the sewer of sin, we must then run and hide in the only truly secure place of our lives. In this secure place we begin to experience the healing of our hurts and health in our hearts. From this hiding place we are able to go out and face the difficulties, even the disasters, of life. From this place we hear the sweet word spoken to the apostle Paul, "My grace is sufficient for you, for My power is perfected in weakness" (2 Corinthians 12:9).

The address of that hiding place is not merely that of a counseling center, a friend, a pastor, or even a spouse. We are secure in this life and in the life to come only through the sufficiency of Jesus Christ.

If you are looking for a temporary easing of the pain inflicted upon you by the disease of sin, you may be tempted to try some of the quick fixes offered by modern psychology and humanistic thinking. However, if you desire to have the deepest needs of your heart met, then you must go to the cross. There you will discover that Jesus, the Messiah, is sufficient to meet every need of your life.

"But," some may protest, "I'm not hurting because of my sin. I'm hurting because of what someone has done to me," or "I'm hurting because of health problems or the death of a loved one. What do I do?"

My response is still the same. Jesus is sufficient to meet every need of your life. To the fatherless, He is "our Father." To the sick, He is the "Great Physician." To the dying, He is "Eternal Life." To those worried about their future, He is the "Alpha and Omega, the Beginning and the End." He is all and in all and capable of meeting the deep hurts of our hearts.

These are not smug little Christian clichés or pious platitudes. I speak as a fellow soldier who has been wounded on the battleground of life. I know the hurts of losing a father to a deadly disease, or a best friend to an automobile accident. I know the hurt of seeing a small son suffer. But I also know the limitless ability of our great God to meet our deepest needs.

Yes, the hurts of life are real. The pain can be excruciating. But our God has totally identified with us. He allowed the worst kind of hurt to be inflicted upon His only begotten Son. Jesus can identify with us. He can weep with us. He has felt what we so often feel. And He says, "Come to Me, all who are weary and heavy-laden, and I will give you rest" (Matthew 11:28).[1]

An Intense Battle

Certainly we are engaged in a battle that can be exhausting as well as devastating. Only Jesus is capable of transforming the human personality and bringing healing to the deep hurts of the human heart.

The battle in which every Christian finds himself engaged can be understood as one pictures a tree. The root of the tree represents the deepest part of the battle, spiritual warfare. The trunk of the tree represents the broadest arena of the battle—the human personality (consisting of mind, will, and emotions). The fruit of the tree represents the most obvious effect of the battle—the moral and spiritual values within the person, which, when tasty and wholesome, should affect society positively.

The battle for the human personality rages with tremendous intensity. If Satan can poison the waters from which the human spirit drinks, then he will ultimately produce human rottenness and depravity within society. But we must realize that the flow of spiritual nutrients (good or bad) from the spirit of man to the moral and spiritual values of society always runs through the human personality. That is why the beliefs, attitudes, and feelings of Christians are so vital to the outcome of the battle. What we believe and how we feel make us salt and light to a tasteless and dark world.

A couple of years before the disintegration of communism in Eastern Europe, I read a stimulating column in the *San Antonio Light*. The syndicated columnist wrote that the great battle between East and West was ideological. He believed that the East was winning the war because the West had no ideology capable of countering the communist worldview.

The journalist's presupposition contained two basic mistakes. First, the writer assumed the communist worldview had power to meet human needs, but it was hollow and incapable of meeting the deepest needs of the human heart. Human beings were reduced to being mere animals with a higher intellect. When the Romanian revolution erupted and Romania's evil dictator was deposed, citizens throughout the nation did something unusual. They cut a hole in the center of the Romanian flag, removing the communist sickle. They took the symbol of communism out of the flag. Everywhere I went throughout the country, flags were flying with holes in the centers. The people were saying, "We have been lied to for four and one half decades. Communism is hollow and meaningless, and we reject its ideology."

We have abandoned biblical beliefs for pagan pluralism. We have adopted a philosophy that says, "It doesn't matter what you believe, as long as you believe in something."

The second mistake that the columnist made was in assuming that the West had no ideology with which to combat communism. Western civilization does have a rich heritage of the Judeo-Christian beliefs and values. It is the biblical belief system upon which the West was built that has given us virtue. However, we have drifted very rapidly the last twenty-five years from the very "ideology" that has made us great in the past. It is not that the West has no great ideology. We have forsaken the very ideology that is the cornerstone upon which a decent society can be constructed.

We have abandoned biblical beliefs for pagan pluralism. We have adopted a philosophy that says, "It doesn't matter what you believe, as long as you believe in something." That something can be Jesus, the Bible, money, yourself, Islam, New Age, or atheism. It really doesn't matter. America has become a melting pot of beliefs. However, our children and grandchildren may one day wake up to realize that we had the wrong symbol flying in the middle of the flag of our hearts. The symbol of pagan pluralism is as shallow and hollow as that of the communists. It will never meet the deep needs of the human heart.

OUR RESPONSE

What should be the response of Christians during these difficult days in which Western society has deserted the faith of our forefathers? First, we must never embrace any ideology that is not rooted in the Word of God. The Bible is a fortress in which the believer can dwell safely when the enemy attacks. It is the only secure foundation upon which to build our lives when the storm clouds cover the skies.

Jesus is the great Psychologist.
. . . He alone is able to meet
our deepest needs.

We should have a great concern about some "Christian psychology" that is more psychology than Christianity. We must be very careful to understand that psychology not built on a biblical worldview will be incapable of meeting the deepest needs of the human personality. Jesus is the great Psychologist. As believers we must see that He alone is able to meet our deepest needs.

During the dark and difficult days of oppression in Romania, I met Titus Mihet, a pastor who had suffered greatly. He lived in poverty. Titus was harassed and maligned because of his faith. His teenage daughter was ridiculed before her classmates. Their circumstances were most difficult, to say the least.

A friend of mine asked the Romanian pastor if Christians were happy under such circumstances. Titus responded, "Only a Christian from the West could ask that question. The issue for us is not happiness. It's obedience to God and glorifying Him with our lives."

That persecuted pastor understood a great truth that believers in the West must come to grips with. Happiness is not what the Christian is to seek. We are to seek His kingdom, His power, and His glory (Matthew 6:13). With that comes His contentment and sense of purpose. Happiness is a by-product of a surrendered life.

The Christian must cry out, "My only hope is You, Lord." It is at that moment that God is able to meet the deep needs of the heart. The scars on the human personality will begin to be healed by the ointment of God's forgiveness and grace. For many years Christians in Eastern Europe had only God as their Counselor. They found Him to be sufficient to meet every need of their lives. They had no counseling centers. They had to be extremely careful about what they said and to whom they spoke. But they found a sanctuary of healing around the throne of grace.

They didn't win battles by conforming their thought patterns to the dark world systems in which they lived. They found healing and victory in the transforming light of God's Word applied to the human personality. We too must understand that shadows of reality will never dispel the darkness that has covered Western society. The darkness will be pierced only by the truth and light of God's Word. In the battle for the human personality, we must never leave the mighty fortress of God's Word and Christ's sufficiency.

One night he (John Welch) rose and went into the next room, where he stayed so long at secret prayer that his wife, fearing he might catch cold, was constrained to rise and follow him, and, as she hearkened, she heard him speak as by interrupted sentences, "Lord, wilt Thou not grant me Scotland?"

John Howie
The Scot Worthies

And My people who are called by My name humble themselves and pray, and seek My face and turn from their wicked ways, then I will hear from heaven, will forgive their sin, and will heal their land.

2 Chronicles 7:14

3

The Battle
for Society

It's perhaps one of the greatest examples of people taking control of their own destiny during this century. In 1989 the people of Romania broke from the bondage of their cruel dictator, Nicolae Ceaucescu; Romanians had been slaves to one of the most oppressive Communist regimes in existence. I have Romanian friends who are willing to show the scars on their bodies inflicted by the dreaded Securitate police, who were trying to silence them. Other friends risked their lives by swimming the Danube River to Yugoslavia to escape the misery imposed by the barbaric dictator. Still others went to prison and simply learned to exist.

Then the revolution exploded without notice. After the secret police fired on Christian men, women, and children, 100,000 people took to the streets of Timisoara, Romania's second largest city. Demonstrations quickly spread throughout the nation, and the military refused to shoot their own people. Within one week the dictator tried to escape the country, but Ceaucescu and his wife were captured and eventually executed by a transitional government. News commentators told the world that it was one of the greatest displays of people power in modern history. But was it? Leaders of the newly formed government declared that they had secretly been planning the revolution all along. Was it people power, a coup d'état, or was there another force at work in setting the captive nation free?

ROMANIA AND THE POWER OF GOD

I have traveled into Romania for almost fifteen years. I have met secretly with Christians in mountain forests and have preached publicly in churches prior to the revolution. I was arrested and deported from the country one and a half years before freedom came to the people. I reentered the country at the close of the revolution. Since then I have spoken to the masses in numerous stadiums throughout the nation. As an eyewitness to these historic events, I am convinced that it was neither people power nor leadership power that delivered the Romanian people from their bondage. *It was God's power.*

I do not make that statement lightly. Nor do I declare it from a Christian bias. Actual historical events point to a divine intervention in Romania's history. The Romanian revolution was a time in which the clouds of fear and atheism were blown out of the country in one divine moment, and courage grew from hearts of faith. With faith the people marched to major plazas of the nation and loosed the chains that held them captive for four and one-half decades.

Fifteen years prior to the revolution a godly pastor, Liviu Olah, began to teach his people in Oradea about the power of a God who answers the prayers of His people. He taught them to pray that one day they would be able to preach the gospel in the great stadiums of the nation. He told them to pray that the gospel would be proclaimed in the newspapers and on television. The people heeded his call and prayed even though it seemed impossible.

The days became darker, but they continued in intercession. Pastor Olah eventually was exiled; yet the people persisted in prayer. For two decades they prayed. They refused to give up. They fought from the position of the bent knee. They had no political clout and were treated as the scum of the earth. These nobodies knew Somebody. That Somebody had all authority in heaven and on earth. They petitioned for two decades that He would shut the mouth of the blasphemers and display His glory to the nation.

That day finally arrived. A Hungarian pastor, Lazlo Tokes, was to be arrested for his outspoken views in the city of Timisoara during December 1989. Members of his church began to gather in front of his apartment to protect him from the dreaded Securitate. Christians from other churches joined in. The air was filled with anticipation. Something big was about to happen. And it did.

The Securitate fired indiscriminately into the crowd, shooting innocent men, women, and children. At that moment, it was as though the wrath and glory of God were simultaneously released from heaven—the wrath of God upon the evil Ceaucescu regime and the glory of God upon His people. The sequence of events that followed suggest that God is very active in the affairs of human history.

Soon much of the crowd picked up the shout, which echoed across the plaza: "Exista Dumnezeu! Exista Dumnezeu!" *("There is a God! There is a God!")*

Tens of thousands of people gathered in the central plaza of the city to protest the atrocities. Peter Dugalescu, pastor of the First Baptist Church, stood among the people and began to proclaim the gospel. As Pastor Dugalescu declared the existence of God, a shout was heard in the crowd, *"Exista Dumnezeu."* Soon much of the crowd picked up the shout, which echoed across the plaza:*"Exista Dumnezeu! Exista Dumnezeu!"* ("There is a God! There is a God!")

They had been taught for forty-five years that God did not exist and were punished for any public expression of their faith. They were brainwashed from kindergarten to postgraduate university with "scientific atheism." But now faith erupted in their hearts, and they exclaimed praises to God. One hundred thousand people knelt with Pastor Dugalescu and repeated the Lord's Prayer. The theme song of the people became a song about the Second Coming of Christ. The explosion of faith spread like a wildfire, and similar scenes occurred in cities throughout the nation. In Bucharest the people had no weapons. They stormed the television station and took it with faith in their hearts. The first words uttered on television by the people startled the nation, *"Dumnezeu este cu noi!"* ("God is with us!")

When I arrived in the country at the close of the revolution, I preached on the streets and people would begin to shout, "There is a God! There is a God!" I have never heard such joyful proclamations during my entire life. A Christian from the nearby city of Arad told me that the people also gathered in the plaza of his city. "The Securitate were in buildings surrounding the tens of thousands that had gathered that evening," he said. "Their guns were pointed at us, and we began to shout, 'God is with us! God is with us!' They could not stand in the face of such faith. They threw their weapons down and ran!"

These events are not to suggest that all of Romania was converted to Christ in one week. Extremely rapid growth is taking place in the church at this time, but many continue to look for the truth; that is the task of the church today—to help them find it. But those demonstrations of faith show that the Romanians' freedom from bondage was conceived in prayer, birthed by the arrest of a Christian pastor, and enlarged by the faith that sprang in the hearts of the people. Unknown believers waged a battle from the secret closet of prayer—and won. They utilized weapons that were awesome but unknown to the political and military leaders of their country.

I am afraid that they are also unknown to many of the Christian leaders in the West. There's a lot of talk about spiritual warfare within the Christian community but very little victory. Technique and technology have replaced the powerful weapons of prayer and purity. The result has been confusion, darkness, apathy, defeat, and a lot of religious hype. My heart breaks when I return from some country where God's Spirit is moving mightily. I come back to America only to discover that another scandal has rocked the Christian community, or another Christian brother or sister has filed for divorce, or someone has been less than truthful about his or her ministry. Finances, church attendance, and technology have replaced humility, purity, and integrity as the hallmark of Christian leadership.

The gospel is relevant. It always has been and always will be relevant. The issue is not "relevancy" but rather "understandability."

In an attempt to become "relevant," the church has found herself compromised with the world she attempts to reach. In *The Frog in the Kettle*, George Barna, president of a marketing research company, does an excellent job defining trends that the church will face in the twenty-first century. He has some very good and practical things to say to church leaders. However, a great concern arises in my heart as I watch Christian leaders jump on the bandwagon of "relevancy." First, the church does not need to make the gospel relevant. The gospel is relevant. It always has been and always will be relevant. The issue is not "relevancy" but rather "understandability" (which we will deal with more thoroughly later). And when the gospel is truly understood, it will divide. Many will hate those who proclaim it while others will bow before the cross and salute the resurrected Savior.

In a section in his book Barna speaks of "Challenges and Opportunities for the Church." He states, "While many of the televangelist ministries have been innovators in technology (Pat Robertson and Oral Roberts have used cutting edge technology for years), the local church has rarely been in the forefront of the movement." He then says that the effective church will be "technologically savvy".[1]

Barna goes on to say, "Some social scientists have argued that the televangelism scandals of the late '80s initiated a downward tumble for Christianity that has yet to be halted. The data, however, do not support this theory. The evidence does indicate that the Jim Bakker and Jimmy Swaggart episodes, in particular, confirmed some negative feelings that many adults previously had about the Christian Church. But there has been no enduring determination to judge the faith in general or local churches in particular on the basis of those circumstances."[2]

TECHNOLOGY AND RELEVANCE

Herein lies my concern. The church is encouraged to become "technologically savvy." Then a deduction is made from marketing research that the church has not been harmed by the scandals of some of those who have been on the cutting edge of communications technology. However, the spiritual atmosphere that has been created by such scandals is unknown, and no research can measure it. It is doubtful that it is strongly positive. Clearly, evangelism and church growth are most conducive in a positive spiritual atmosphere. The greatest evangelistic harvests biblically and historically have come during times of revival. Revival is a time when the spiritual atmosphere of a local church, community, or a nation is charged with God's presence. The instruments of revival have always been men and women whose lives have been surrendered to God. They have not been perfect, but they have certainly been committed to a life of moral purity.

For example, the meetings in Norilsk, Siberia, were some of the most unusual that I have ever conducted. Thousands came to the stadium that first evening that I preached. Their interest was genuine; you could have heard a pin drop in the stadium. Prior to the meeting there were only forty Christians. After presenting a straightforward gospel presentation, I challenged those listening to repent of their sins and place their faith in Christ. The response was overwhelming. Ninety-five percent of those in attendance came forward saying that they had chosen to follow Christ. I had seen wonderful responses to the message of Christ in the former Soviet Union. But I had never seen anything comparable to this in more than two decades of international evangelism.

At the conclusion of the services in Norilsk I was interviewed by a local journalist who asked me a very interesting question. She said, "Many people here believe that our city is cursed because of the slave labor that built the city. Do you agree with that assessment?"

"I believe just the opposite is true," I answered. The response to the message of Christ had been incredible. Many of those who died in the slave labor camps were Christians. I believe that many of those godly men prayed for this day. And the heavenly Father holds dear to His heart the blood of the martyrs. The blessings that we have experienced today have perhaps resulted from the prayers of those who suffered for Christ."

Those persecuted believers had no technology in their spiritual armory, but they did have weapons with which no government or dictator could contend. They left behind a spiritual atmosphere in which God could intervene in the affairs of their community. They were far from being perfect, but there was a line drawn in the sand of their hearts. They had stepped across that line to say, "I'll follow Christ , no matter what the cost."

There is nothing wrong with a church being "technologically savvy." But that in no way ensures the effectiveness of a church. Just the opposite can be true. The church that is "technologically savvy" but has no deep commitment to holiness, humility, integrity, and prayer can do great damage in the kingdom of God, both locally and internationally. Barna says that recent scandals have only "confirmed some negative feelings that many adults previously held about the Christian church." However, those adults are the very people that need to be reached with the gospel. This is no time for the status quo. We must penetrate the darkest areas of our society with the message of Christ. The hardest hearts can and must be melted by the power of God's Spirit.

The apostle Paul was a man with confirmed negative attitudes toward the local church (to say the least). However, I don't think that if Paul were living in the twenty-first century he would respond to the technological savvy of televangelists who have no deep commitments to integrity or moral purity. I believe that he would respond to the same kind of witnessing that ultimately brought him to Christ in the first century. Perhaps the most influential factor of his coming to Christ prior to his Damascus Road experience was the martyrdom of Stephen. He saw the glory of God in the eyes of Stephen. I believe that it haunted him until that traumatic moment on the Damascus Road. Technique would never have reached Paul. But men and women who lived for nothing but the glory of God shook Paul to the core. The darkness that dwelt for so many years in his heart was pierced by the light of Christian soldiers, followers of Christ who knew God's mighty weapons for battle were not physical, but spiritual and "divinely powerful for the destruction of fortresses" (2 Corinthians 10:4). We must likewise understand that the battle the church is facing lies in a spiritual dimension and will only be won on God's terms as dictated in His Word.

Much of the essence of the gospel has been lost to a slick, commercialized Jesus presented by wealthy evangelists shedding crocodile tears. I have traveled to many of the unevangelized areas of the world to proclaim light to people whose hearts are engulfed in darkness. The greatest hindrance to the understandability of the gospel had been the lifestyle of some of my fellow evangelists who see themselves as superstars rather than God's servants.

The gospel is made understandable as it becomes reality in the lives of God's people. The uniqueness of Jesus lies in the historical fact that He is Almighty God who became a man. He's the king who became a servant. He's not a religious success. He's just the opposite. If the nature of Christ is to be understood in a dark world, then we must represent Him as servants rather than celebrities.

While preaching in Durban, South Africa, I had some frank discussions with Ahmed Deedat, a Muslim leader and director of a center of evangelism for Islam, which is the world's fastest growing religion. Deedat proclaimed that Islam had triumphed over Christianity. His proof? He had debated Jimmy Swaggart immediately prior to Swaggart's being exposed for the first time for a visit to a prostitute. He saw Swaggart's scandal as Allah's judgment on "the Christian West." After discussions with Deedat and a couple of his loyal followers, I became convinced that the darkness of Islam will not be penetrated merely by the strong influence of technology. The very technology that many Christians have hailed as the means of reaching the unreached has become the source of ridicule and hardening of the hearts of one of the neediest groups of people in the world. It is the life wholly yielded to the Holy Spirit that will break the stronghold of Islam or any other false religion. God has not changed. His message becomes understandable not by technique but through transformed lives.

Television or technology are neither right nor wrong. They are simply tools that can be used properly or improperly. But we must never forget that God has never promised to bless machines. He could have created robots. But he didn't. He created you and me, living souls. He has promised to use people, common ordinary people. People whose lives are surrendered to God become a mighty weapon in God's arsenal. The darkness can be penetrated by lives that reflect the light of Jesus Christ.

But some of my colleagues may protest saying, "That's fine. We need holy living. But if we are going to reach the world we must do it with twenty-first-century methods and not nineteenth-century ones."

There's nothing wrong with that line of reasoning—at first glance. For instance, John Wesley rode thousands of miles on horseback to set the fires of revival throughout Britain. God used him in a mighty way to bring thousands into the kingdom as well as affect change in the moral climate of his generation. If Wesley were alive today there's no doubt in my mind that he would be jetting around the globe to bring the gospel to some unreached people group. His brother, Charles, would probably be working with a notebook computer to write the great hymns inspired in his heart by God.

However, a subtle temptation exists to become dependent upon a method of God rather than upon the God of the method. For instance, an undue focus on technology would have John Wesley holding seminars around the world on how to become technologically savvy. But Wesley would never have conducted lectures on "Horseback Riding and Evangelism." His heart was somewhere else.

Bishop J. C. Ryle's description of Wesley tells us what he would probably be doing and saying in these dark days. Ryle says, "He was a bold fighter on Christ's side, a fearless warrior against sin, the world and the devil, and an unflinching adherent of the Lord Jesus Christ in a very dark day. He honored the Bible. He cried down sin. He made much of Christ's blood. He exalted holiness. He taught the absolute need of repentance, faith, and conversion. Surely these things ought not to be forgotten."[3]

As television (even Christian television) often emphasizes image and appearance over content, Christians can easily be led into a walk of sight and not faith.

The methods of God change from culture to culture and generation to generation, but the Word of God never changes. His truth alone can dispel the darkness. A commitment to God is a commitment to build our lives on the authority of His Word. Technology is simply a method, an instrument in modern society. It does not hold any supernatural powers.

The fight will be won on the battlefield of the human heart and not the arena of talent and technology. The battle originates in the deepest part of the human heart—the spirit of man. It then moves into the arena of the human personality. But it ultimately leaves its effect upon society. Christians must realize that we become the very instruments of God to change society when our lives are surrendered to Christ. We must understand that we actually become God's method of effecting change.

Television is one piece of technology that must be handled with extreme care. The post-World War II baby boomer generation has grown up with it. It has become one of the most powerful influences known to mankind. During the Romanian revolution the television station became the center of the conflict. Both sides knew the power in the station to determine the future of their nation. Because of this kind of influence, many Christians believe that the darkness in our society will only be pierced through the use of this instrument.

However, we must remember that television can be deceptive and lead to error. It is built upon sight principles rather than faith principles. The Christian "walks by faith, not by sight" (2 Corinthians 5:7). And faith "comes from hearing, and hearing by the word of Christ" (Romans 10:17). The faith principle is rooted in truth. Content is of utmost importance. The sight principle is not rooted in truth, only the appearance of it. Presentation often takes precedence over content. As television (even Christian television) often emphasizes image and appearance over content, Christians can easily be led into a walk of sight and not faith. We must handle TV with extreme caution.

I first understood this when I visited Universal Studios in Hollywood. I was amazed to see what a camera could do to reality. Small models of spacecraft were made to appear as 2,000-foot vehicles. Illusion quickly became reality, and reality gave way to illusion. I think I understood what Paul meant when he wrote to the church at Thessalonica, "God will send them a deluding influence so they might believe what is false" (2 Thessalonians 2:11). Today an entire generation has grown up shaping their moral values and belief system based upon the principle of sight rather than faith.

This isn't true only for secular television, but also for Christian television. A great tragedy has occurred since freedom was gained in Eastern Europe. Many Western Christians have taken their video cameras and returned giving the impression of a deep burden for people for whom they have never wept. They have discovered the powerful influence of television, but have themselves become victims of its deceptive influence. One day I was asked by a nationally known televangelist for video footage of our first crusade in the former Soviet Union. The evangelist/ TV host was in the midst of financial difficulties. His ministry decided to go to the Soviet Union and needed to raise funds. They heard about our ministry and what we had accomplished. They wanted to use our video footage in the United States to promote their Soviet crusades.

Hollywood is built upon superstars. Christianity is built upon servants.

This kind of deceptive use of Christian television has convinced me that much of the Christian community has been mistaken about its powerful influence. TV appeals not only to our sight but also to our desire for self gratification. Hollywood is built upon superstars. Christianity is built upon servants. The two principles are contrary to one another. A person cannot maintain the status of a star and live in the trenches as a lowly servant at the same time. It's true that a person can become an egoist without appearing on television. It's also true that a person can have a television ministry and be a humble servant of God. But Christians must be extremely careful to avoid the perilous pitfalls of television ministry. Television caters to performers. In contrast, revival is an expression of the grace of God. That grace can only be applied to a heart of humility.

But most important, the church must give serious thought to how we can most effectively influence our generation for Christ. We must never become dependent on technique or technology. Certain tools can be utilized well in our modern culture, but let's never be deceived about the true source of power. God still works through humble, holy, praying men and women. We must return to the age-old principles recorded in the Word of God. They are time-tested and have proven reliable.

I would certainly agree that we should use the available film and electronic technology to reach a world that has never heard the message of Christ. For instance, Campus Crusade for Christ has done an excellent job of distributing the film *Jesus*, a movie based on the life of Christ as recorded in the Gospel of Luke. It has been translated into more than 170 languages and presented to more than 500 million people. It is available on video cassette for viewing in the home, where families and neighbors can gather. I can only say, "To God be the glory for such an effort."

But we must remember that no one can come to Christ unless there is a deep work of the Holy Spirit in the human heart. The Holy Spirit normally speaks through three channels. First, He speaks through the message of the gospel. Paul said, "For Christ did not send me to baptize, but to preach the gospel, not in cleverness of speech, that the cross of Christ should not be made void. For the word of the cross is to those who are perishing foolishness, but to us who are being saved it is the power of God. And my message and my preaching were not in persuasive words of wisdom, but in demonstration of the Spirit and of power" (1 Corinthians 1:17–18; 2:4). There is something extraordinary about presenting the gospel verbally, visually, or in written form. Through the message of Christ the Holy Spirit can penetrate the darkest heart.

Also, God speaks through creation. Paul says, "For since the creation of the world His invisible attributes, His eternal power and divine nature, have been clearly seen, being understood through what has been made, so that they are without excuse" (Romans 1:20). All of creation declares the glory of God.

A university student in Leningrad to whom I had witnessed about Christ in the early seventies once told me, "I have never believed in God. But two weeks ago I was looking into the heavens, and I began to wonder if God existed. The universe is so orderly and I thought that this could not have happened by chance. So I prayed and said, 'God, if you exist, would you reveal yourself to me?' He answered my prayer by sending you here to tell me about Christ."

I was overwhelmed by what I heard. The Holy Spirit declared the glory of God to a young atheist through creation. Then He sent someone to speak to him the message of Christ. When both creation speaks and the message of Christ are presented clearly, there is unlimited potential to see lives transformed.

A Holy Life

But when a third element is added to the equation, the potential release of God's power is multiplied even more. That element is a holy life: "For the eyes of the Lord move to and fro throughout the earth that He may strongly support those whose heart is completely His" (2 Chronicles 16:9a). I am convinced that the liberation of Romania to hear the gospel came from humble, holy, praying men and women in that nation. They prayed and God moved an entire nation.

The Moldavian young people who traveled with us to the far north of Siberia spoke of their forefathers. Many of them had been shipped to Siberian gulags by dictatorial communist regimes. They were awed now to be able to stand on the same ground where their grandfathers had died for the sake of Christ. Yet they were able to proclaim publicly the message of Christ. They believed that it was the blood of their martyred forefathers that cried to heaven for the day the Siberian people could hear the message of Christ.

Nations will be changed and history rewritten when the Holy Spirit has access to all three channels: creation, the spoken message of Christ, and lives surrendered to God. The most powerful weapon for impacting society for Christ is the transformed life.

Of course, the call to change may not be popular in an age when the church is being taught to cater to the baby boomers. I am a post-World War II baby boomer and I can honestly say that my generation doesn't need to be "catered to." That may be what we want, but it's not what we need. We need to experience death to self. The message of Christ to our generation may not be popular, but it's absolutely necessary. He said, "He who loves his life loses it; and he who hates his life in this world shall keep it to eternal life" (John 12:25).

My generation made a conscious decision to throw out traditional values and biblical morality. Now we are feeling the effects of our sin within society. Before there will ever be the healing of this hurting generation, we must repent of our self-centered lifestyles. We must return to old-time, old-fashioned biblical principles upon which we can build our lives. That process must begin deep within the heart of every believer. Then our light will shine brightly into a dark and unbelieving generation.

Part 2
The Character of the Soldier

In any situation where Satan dominates and threatens, God looks for a man through whom He may declare war on the enemy. He purposes that through this man Satan be served notice to back up, pack up, and clear out.

Arthur Matthews
Born for Battle

For the eyes of the Lord move to and fro throughout the earth that He may strongly support those whose heart is completely His.

2 Chronicles 16:9

4

The Soldier's Character

The Ukrainian pastor came rushing into the hotel and grabbed me. "Sammy, we have big problems!" he exclaimed. "The general over the military has torn up our contract to use the stadium tonight and tomorrow. Thousands of people have our invitations to come to the stadium and will be there. What can we do?" Then he looked at me anxiously and said, "Sammy, our only hope is for you to talk to the general."

"You've got to be kidding!" I exclaimed. "If I'm the only hope, then our problems are bigger than you think. I'm a simple preacher. That general won't listen to me."

"But we must try," he said.

We gathered the team to pray while I went to talk to the general. But my reasoning proved correct. The general wouldn't even speak with me. We were left with only one other alternative—prayer. So, we spent the rest of the morning seeking God. The situation looked bleak. It was two months prior to the attempted coup by hard-core communists to overthrow Mikhail Gorbachev. In the Ukraine, as elsewhere, many leaders in the Soviet military were uneasy with the new freedoms that were coming to their country, especially the religious freedoms.

It seemed as though all of our money, energy, time, and effort put into such an evangelistic mission were for nothing.

Then God intervened. A colonel in the Soviet military felt very bad about what had happened to us. He came to us and said, "I will try to help you. There's another stadium in the city. It's not as large, but I think it will be adequate. I'll speak with the city council about using that stadium. Normally it takes three to four months to obtain permission. But I will try."

To our utter amazement the colonel obtained permission at great risk to his own position. (I recently learned that he mysteriously died in an accident a few weeks after our departure.) Regardless of the cost to his own life, he put his troops on the streets, redirecting the thousands of people coming to the previous stadium. The military sent them to the other stadium that we had permission to use.

We were giving God praise for His provision—until we walked out of our hotel. Rain was pouring down, and my heart sank. No one would come to the stadium in such a downpour. I prayed the whole way to the stadium. Again I was surprised. It was raining everywhere in the city except the vicinity of the stadium that had just been secured. I really began to rejoice when I saw a dry stadium filled with thousands of people. That night hundreds of people came to Christ.

The next three weeks were to become the most fruitful ever in my ministry. Night after night we saw thousands come to Christ. It was a most unusual time. We spoke in several unreached cities in the Ukraine and Romania. Every morning we woke up to pouring rain. We spent most every day in prayer asking God to stop the rain and to bring people to the stadiums to hear the message of Christ. God was not under obligation to do that, but in His grace He granted our petitions.

A CARPET AND A LESSON IN CHARACTER

While in both cities, I also decided to purchase some rugs for back home. We had just put wood floors in our Texas home. The Soviet Union and Romania had beautiful Oriental-style rugs that could be purchased very inexpensively. So, I purchased one carpet in Romania and another in the Ukraine. The Romanian carpet was my favorite.

But when we attempted to leave Romania a customs agent said that I could not bring both carpets out of the country. I could take the Soviet carpet but must leave behind the Romanian one.

I showed the agent our export documents and receipts. But nothing satisfied him. The Romanian carpet had to stay. I was really disappointed. But one of the team members had an idea. He said, "Sammy, the agent didn't look at the carpet closely. He only saw the tags on the back of them. We could just switch the tags, and he would never know the difference. Then you could bring the Romanian carpet out and leave the Ukrainian one here."

The world looks for people of strength, power, wealth, and youthfulness for its soldiers. God is looking for men and women who are growing in Christlike character.

I must be honest with you. It sounded like a brilliant idea, and I seriously considered doing it. But about that time another team member wisely spoke up, "Sammy, I'll bet you could get that Romanian carpet out of the country right now. But the next time you ask God to stop the rain, I'll bet He doesn't do it."

It was as though somebody slapped me in the face. Conviction pierced my heart. I couldn't believe that I was about to trade power in prayer for an old piece of carpet. Our successes in the Ukraine and Romania were due largely to God's interceding to withhold the rain. He blessed our ministry in response to fervent prayers and clean hearts. Now I was about to trade spiritual health for a piece of carpet. And that is exactly what so many of us have done. Many believers, seeking convenience over personal growth have kept secret sins in the hidden crevasses of their hearts. They've thought, "Nobody will know, and, besides, it's not hurting anyone but me."

Nothing could be further from the truth. Western civilization is quickly being plunged into moral and spiritual darkness. Only a great awakening will turn the tide of society from moral depravity to biblical values. But such a revival will only come through a mighty prayer movement. The Scriptures say, "The effective prayer of a righteous man can accomplish much" (James 5:16). A "righteous man" refers to our position in Christ. We can come boldly to God in spite of past sins because we have been clothed with Christ's righteousness. But it also refers to practical righteousness. As we surrender our lives to Christ daily, we experience the outworking of the indwelling righteousness of Christ. We commonly call it *character*.

The world looks for people of strength, power, wealth, and youthfulness for its soldiers. God is looking for men and women who are growing in Christlike character. When he finds such a man or woman hidden away in the private place of prayer, He will move heaven and earth to change the course of history.

Character is of utmost importance in the life of the soldier on the battlefield under Christ's command. It places him right in the middle of God's eternal purposes. Paul stated that such a soldier has been predestined "to become conformed to the image of His Son, that He might be the firstborn among many brethren" (Romans 8:29b). It's not that the soldier has achieved complete conformity that makes him usable in piercing the darkness of a godless society. No soldier has ever obtained such conformity in his lifetime. But the man or woman who lives on the cutting edge of conformity to Christ becomes an awesome weapon in combating the darkness.

The goal of the soldier must be to grow each day more into the image of Christ. Satan is aware of the tremendous strength in God's arsenal when a soldier of Christ commits his life to becoming all that God wants him to be. William Gurnall said, "As an earthly parent you rejoice to see your own good qualities reproduced in your children. God, the perfect parent, longs to see His attributes reflected in His saints. *It is this image reflected in you that so enrages hell; it is this at which the demons hurl their mightiest weapons*"[1] (emphasis added).

CHARISMA VERSUS CHARACTER

The Western church has become more concerned with talent and ability rather than character and integrity. We have too often exalted people into leadership because of personal charisma rather than inner character. The church in Eastern Europe survived some of the worst assaults in the history of Christendom because Christians there held to a standard of holiness of life during the darkest days of the battle. They were not quick to baptize new converts in order to publicize their church growth. Their heroes were men and women who stood unflinchingly for Christ in the face of the greatest difficulties. They didn't have Christian bookstores, Christian television and radio, nor a lot of superstars in their spiritual arsenal. But they did have simple, humble men and women who desired first and foremost to honor Christ with their lives. (However, there is great danger today with the influx of Western Christians that the church in Eastern Europe may forget the true source of its strength. I pray that this does not happen.)

When freedoms first began to come to Eastern Europe, I preached a national evangelistic meeting in Moldavia, then still a republic of the Soviet Union. After preaching on national television, I was called into the office of the mayor of the capital city, Kishinev. I didn't know what to expect because I had been arrested for preaching the gospel in Leningrad several years earlier. However, I was surprised at what Mayor Nicolai Kostin told me. "We have persecuted the Christians," said Kostin, who is also a member of the Moldavian Parliament. "We have treated them as the scum of the earth, as the dirt on the floor. And we were wrong. The very morality that we need to make our society function properly is that of the Christians." What an admission! Even though the communists opposed the Christian church, they could not deny the light of their holy lives. The believers had little education and ability, but they had the light of Christlike character that was undeniable.

Our battle is with Satan and the demonic forces of hell. He can disguise himself very easily with talent and ability, but not with Christlikeness. In his book *Great Leaders of the 18th Cen-*

tury, J. C. Ryle describes the the work of revivalist William Grimshaw. One day a lady told Grimshaw about a minister who impressed her with his great talent, though she admitted the man had little character.

"Madam," Grimshaw said, "I'm glad you never saw the devil. He has greater talents than all the ministers in the world. I fear, if you saw him, you would fall in love with him, as you have so high a regard of talents without sanctity. Pray, do not be led away with the sound of talents."[2]

Search the Scriptures. You will find the men and women most used of God to break the stronghold of Satan were men and women yielded to God. When they were not yielded to Him, they were powerless over the ancient foe. The same stands true throughout the history of the church. God continues to look for lives surrendered to Him. A great turning point in the life of the great nineteenth-century evangelist D. L. Moody came when Henry Varley said to him in passing, "The world has not yet seen what God can do through a man wholly yielded to Him." Moody determined in his heart to be such a man. As a result, Moody shook two continents for the glory of God. Where are such men and women in this great moment in the history of the church?

But you may protest, saying, "I'm no apostle Paul, D. L. Moody, or any other great saint. I'm not really sure that I can be the kind of person about whom you are speaking."

If those are your thoughts, then you are correct—and incorrect! The first step in becoming like Christ is recognizing your own inability to conform your life into His image. At that moment, cast yourself upon His grace to make you more like Christ each day. You will discover the need of daily and even moment-by-moment dependence upon God's grace. His grace will always prove to be sufficient to conform you into the image of Christ.

The great teacher/author Andrew Murray said, "A life of absolute surrender has its difficulties. I do not deny that. Yes, it has something far more than difficulties: it is a life that with men is absolutely impossible. But by the grace of God, by the power of the Holy Spirit dwelling in us, it is a life to which we are destined, and a life that is possible for us, praise God! Let us believe that God will maintain it."[3]

GODLY CHARACTER

How do we become people of Christlike character? First, we must understand what conformity into the image of Christ means. It's not perfectionism. It doesn't mean that all of a sudden you are some great man or woman of God that never has to deal with sin or failure. Conformity unto the image of Christ is a lifelong process. As we surrender daily to Christ, God continues His work of grace in the heart of the believer. As we continue to surrender to Christ, we come to understand how unlike Him we really are. We comprehend how much more we need to surrender to Christ. We are the least likely to recognize our own growth. And the signs, or fruit, that we are on the highway of conformity to Christlike character will become more apparent to two others: God and other people. As a result, we become God's weapon to penetrate the darkness in other lives.

Not only must we recognize the nature of godly character, but we must also live with a keen sense of eternal accountability. I have traveled into numerous cultures. Without exception, I have noticed that a lack of accountability always leads to corruption in society. Recently in Texas a number of savings institutions closed. Some of the failures were attributed to dishonesty. A friend of mine worked as a certified public accountant at one of those banks. "I learned one thing through all of this," he said. "If it is in the heart of a person to cheat, he will somehow devise a way to do it. We had a whole team of professionals trained to prevent such a thing from happening. But if someone is determined to steal from the system, he will go to any extreme to do it."

I thought about what he said in light of what is happening today in the Western church. Many Christians have lost a sense in their hearts that one day they will have to give an account of their lives to God. It has resulted in immorality and abuse among some of our best-known leaders. And I'm genuinely concerned that what has been exposed is only the tip of the iceberg.

Part of the reason that we have lost much of our credibility in society is because we have ceased living in the light of eternity. We have little concern for those without Christ because we have subconsciously developed a system of "evangelical universalism." We say that we believe in hell and eternal punishment, but we no longer preach the age-old truth. We act as though everyone will eventually make it to heaven, as though salvation will be universal. We claim that one day we will give an account of our every thought, word, and deed to a holy God. But we live as though that day will never come.

THE IMPACT OF ETERNITY

During the dark days of the evil Romanian dictator Ceascescu, I was severely rebuked by a Romanian Christian friend. He was highly educated and had traveled much with me. He asked me, "Why is it that I have never heard a message on hell from any of the preachers from the West who come here to preach? Why have I never heard you preach on hell? Do you believe in hell?"

"Of course I do," I defended myself. "But the gospel is positive. It's good news! And I want to be a positive proclaimer of the good news."

My friend didn't let me off the hook. "I don't think that you fully understand the nature of the wrath and justice of God," he said. "These attributes of God are very important to us in Eastern Europe. Without understanding those traits you will never be able to grasp how really good the good news is! And you will lose a sense of eternal accountability. That will lead to spiritual impotence and moral failure."

When I returned to the United States, I made a thorough search of the Scriptures as well as my own heart and motives. My friend is correct. We reside in a culture that lives for the moment. The church has conformed much of its theology and behavior to that kind of philosophy. The results have been devastating.

During the Easter season of 1992, John Patten, Secretary of State for Education in England, made a statement that rocked his nation and provoked much debate among journalists. "Faith provided a bedrock for civil behavior," he said. "Dwindling belief in redemption and damnation has lead to loss of fear of the eternal consequences of goodness and badness. It has had a profound effect on personal morality, especially on criminality."

John MacLeod, the "Scottish Young Journalist of the Year," devoted an entire editorial to Patten's statements. He laid the blame right at the door of the Christian church. He wrote, "These are strange times in little Britain. Times in which our national churches have abandoned historic Christian doctrine to trumpet the values of redeeming government, even as our rulers decry the role of the saviour-state and enthusiastically preach the power of damnation. . . . Who, Mr. Patten apart, preaches hell today? Why, scarcely a church in the land."[4]

Christian growth comes from daily abandonment to the will and control of God. The more one surrenders to Christ, the more he or she grows.

MacLeod then named specific churches and leaders, including evangelicals who have ceased preaching that grand old doctrine. I believe that Patten and MacLeod were both correct in their observations. Not only has the lack of belief in eternal accountability impacted our Western culture, but it has also left the church powerless in such strategic times. We must not only begin to confront men and women with their eternal destiny, but we must also understand that we are living for eternal values and rewards. When I came to grips with my own eternal answerability, I began to live with a deeper sense of responsibility and urgency—responsibility for my attitudes and actions and urgency to reach men and women for Christ.

When we have purposed in our hearts to live with a keen sense of eternity as the center of our hearts, we will be constrained to surrender our lives wholly to God. This surrender draws us closer in the quest to be more like Christ. It's also the great need of the church in this critical hour of history. More than one hundred years ago, while speaking in Scotland, Andrew Murray asked a godly Christian worker what was the great need of the Christian church. In a simple and very determined manner the man answered, "Absolute surrender to God is the one thing."[5] If absolute surrender to God was so vital then, how much more indispensable is it in this crucial moment of history.

It is essential that we understand what a life surrendered to God really is. Complete surrender isn't the same thing as Christian maturity. Maturity results from a lifetime of Christian growth. Christian growth comes from daily abandonment to the will and control of God. The more one surrenders to Christ, the more he or she grows. The more the person grows, the more he or she recognizes the need to relinquish oneself to Christ. When I first received Christ in my life, I surrendered to Him all that I knew to give to Him. That produced growth in my life. Growth generated a greater responsibility of surrender. I understood more of the character and nature of God. Therefore, I needed to surrender more of myself to God.

Moses and the children of Israel are great examples of this truth. An entire generation of God's people wasn't allowed into the land because they held tightly to sin in their lives. They missed out on the great promise of God because of idolatry, immorality, rebellion against authority, grumbling, and a craving for evil things (1 Corinthians 10:6–10). But Moses wasn't allowed into the Promised Land because he struck a rock rather than speaking to it—a simple lack of faith (Numbers 20: 10–12).

How God treated Moses and how He treated the children of Israel might seem disproportionate. We may have the tendency to think, "The children of Israel deserved what they received. But, poor Moses, he didn't do anything so really bad. He should have been allowed into the Promised Land." But Moses had experienced the holiness of God on the mountain in the Midianite desert. The children of Israel hadn't. Moses knew a greater measure of grace; therefore, he had a greater responsibility to abdicate himself to God.

COMMITMENT VERSUS SURRENDER

The making of a man or woman of God takes a lifetime of daily surrender to God. As a soldier surrenders daily to the commander-in-chief, he will discover a fresh measure of grace to spread the light of Christ in a dark world. We must know that even our surrender won't make us like Christ. Our surrender simply places us in a position to receive grace. One who surrenders to God is saying simply, "I can't live the way I ought to live. Therefore, I abandon myself to You, O God." Surrender is different from commitment. Commitment says, "I'm going to do something for God." But surrender says, "I can't live the life the way Christ would have me to live. I give up. You take control."

Someone asked a Romanian Christian friend who lived for a period of time in the West, "Why have Christians in the West lost their power to penetrate society with the gospel?"

"Western Christians have ceased using the concept of *the surrendered life*," he responded. "They have substituted it with *the committed life*. Commitment emphasizes what man must do. Surrender emphasizes that man is no longer in control. God rules in the heart of man. It's now His responsibility to make us like Christ."

That heart attitude places the soldier of Christ at the disposal of the grace and power of God. His grace is sufficient and His power ample to conform us into the image of Christ. Therefore, the position of the soldier is that of faith and dependence. It's the only location where God's grace can take root and grow. The heart of the soldier must beat with a passion that cries to God, "Without You, I can do nothing, but by your grace I can and will become all that you desire me to be."

The demons of hell will tremble at men and women who have placed themselves at God's disposal. Those soldiers will find themselves on the front lines of this great spiritual conflict. They will lead the charge against the forces of darkness. For light will burst forth from their own lives—the light of Christlike character. Grace will be at the very root of their lives, while character will blossom as their fruit. And they will go forth like a mighty army, capturing hearts and lives for Christ.

The deepest secrets of the Godhead in the fellowship of the Father and Son by the Holy Spirit were to be shown in the family. . . . Look to God as the author of your family life; count upon Him to give all that is needed to make it what it should be.

Andrew Murray
How to Raise Your Children for Christ

For this cause a man shall leave his father and mother, and shall cleave to his wife; and the two shall become one flesh. This mystery is great; but I am speaking with reference to Christ and the church.

Ephesians 5:31–32

5

The Soldier's Family

The stories of James, Carl, and Oscar (not their real names), all Christians, have surprise endings. Here they are.

Southern Louisiana, 1968: "At the close of my testimony the entire public high school student body stood giving a rousing round of applause. It was an overwhelming experience." James, who had become a Christian through my ministry at age fourteen, had a heart burning to reach his fellow students with the gospel, and for the next two years he effectively impacted his campus for Christ. Many of his friends came to a personal faith in Jesus Christ in this predominantly nonevangelical area of the United States.

During the next couple of years, God used James in a tremendous way to reach young people. One weekend almost two hundred youths came to Christ through his preaching. His future looked bright. If he had such results as a teenager, what would happen as he grew older in his Christian faith? Later he met and married a wonderful Christian girl. They had two beautiful children. He became youth pastor at one of America's megachurches.

I think I understood a little of what the apostle John meant when he said, "I have no greater joy than this, to hear of my children walking in the truth." But that joy in my heart did not live long. A few years later James sat across from me in a restaurant trying to explain that he had fallen in love with another woman. I was crushed. I pleaded with him to break off the relationship and return to his wife. I said that I would do anything to help him restore his marriage. He refused to listen. And I wept.

San Antonio, Texas; 1974: Carl and I had never met, but we maintained a mutual respect for one another. Carl had been mightily used of God. He packed civic arenas throughout the southern United States. Tens of thousands not only came to hear him preach, but thousands also responded to give their hearts to Christ.

Finally, the day came when we could personally become acquainted. We sat in the restaurant discussing and dreaming of reaching the world for Christ. We both agreed that nothing was too difficult. The task of world evangelization was altogether possible. But then he made a statement that triggered some concern in my heart. "One of the great obstacles to evangelism today is all of the emphasis being placed on the family. I don't think that it was meant to be a hindrance, but it has become one," he said emphatically. "My great fear is that the importance placed on family life in the Christian community will replace the priority of evangelism in the church."

Almost ten years later I watched his weekly Christian television broadcast. He had begun a church, and it quickly became one of America's fastest growing evangelical churches with almost 10,000 people attending services. That night he spoke of a great spiritual encounter with God that he had recently experienced.

"The Holy Spirit came upon me and knocked me down. I couldn't move," he stated. He continued to describe the experience in mystical terms.

I told my wife, "I'm concerned about Carl. He's in trouble."

"Why do you think that?" she asked.

"My reasons may sound oversimplistic," I said. "But if a person has such a dramatic experience with God, then it will affect his entire personality and life. But he never mentioned one area of his life that was changed because of this encounter.

He couldn't tell how he became a better husband or father. He did not specify one area of his life that changed."
My concern proved correct. Not long after that, he left his wife for another woman.
Fort Worth, Texas; *1982*: Almost 15,000 attended the conference. But I felt all alone. I desperately was looking for answers in my life and ministry. I had known Christ for seventeen years. I had seen many come to Christ over the years. But I found myself struggling. In that moment a friend out of the past, Oscar, walked up to me.
"Sammy, it has been years since I've seen you. How have you been? What are you doing these days?"
I told him of my struggles, and I'll never forget his encouragement. He had been my role model in the ministry. He had gone to the darkest areas of the world with the light of the gospel. He was courageous for Christ. I was deeply moved that a man of his fortitude would take the time to pray with me and help me in my struggles. It made me admire him that much more.
That's why I was heartbroken almost ten years later because he too had left his wife for another woman.
I wish that I could say that the above stories were the only tragedies of friends of which I am aware. But they are only a few of the spiritual catastrophies that have crossed my path over the past several years. All had some common characteristics. As far as I could tell, each of these men had a genuine passion for Christ and a great desire to impact his world for Him. But each also, had misplaced zeal and priorities in his life. Ministry took precedence over marriage. For each man, his cause outgrew his character.
As I observed those men's lives, the following common characteristics seemed obvious to me.

1. They began their Christian walk with a deep desire to penetrate the darkness so prevalent in society.
2. They were gifted and innovative communicators.

3. Building a ministry took priority over building godly character at some point in their Christian experience.
4. At that time they became easy prey for Satan's attack. His strategy was clearly aimed at the destruction of their homes.
5. The quality of their impact upon society was greatly diminished after they yielded to sin.

One might tend to think that the preceding tragedies indicate that the moral problem in the church is confined to male leaders. Not true. In each instance the "other woman" was a Christian. Temptation to immorality is no respecter of the sexes. Women are equally vulnerable. Each of the women involved had six common traits:

1. Each woman seemed to have a sincere desire to serve Christ. In fact, two of them attempted to serve Christ with the men before and after the breakup of their families. They were no different from the men in their desire to be servants of Christ.
2. Each woman had great admiration for the Christian leader's commitment and service to Christ.
3. Each was willing to listen to the dreams and aspirations of the leader. She allowed him to communicate his deepest feelings with her.
4. Their involvement with the men began as an emotional entanglement rather than sensual lust.
5. There were some deep unmet needs in their own lives that opened the women to yielding to the temptation.
6. At some point in the relationship, the women allowed their feelings to overcome their commitment to obey the Scripture.

I don't believe that either the men or the women in the preceding stories entered into their wrong relationships intentionally. I believe that those relationships developed without spiritual discernment, moral boundaries, and a shortage of inward character and maturity. They wanted to *do right* without understanding that they must first *be right* with God. However, the work of God. will be accomplished effectively only as we become all that He wants us to become. That means focusing on developing Christlike character.

CHARACTER AND THE FAMILY

Christlike character in the life of the believer is foundational if we are to penetrate the darkness that exists in society. The real test of our character normally comes within the context of family life. It's easy to impress people who don't know us well; it's much more difficult to wear a mask of super spirituality around our family. Normally they know what we are really like on the inside and outside. Most of the time religious masks don't often fool anyone at home. I've discovered that it's much easier to preach and teach about God's love than it is to live in a Christlike manner with my wife and children.

There must be a revival of the priority of family life if there will ever be a general revival within society.

The family sits at the epicenter of the battle for this generation. To pierce the darkness in Western civilization, the light of the gospel must shine brightly in Christian homes throughout Western Europe and North America. But it appears that the Christian family is struggling for survival as much as the non-Christian family. I believe that there are three basic reasons Christians have struggled to find victory in their own homes during this needy and strategic moment.

First, we have had misplaced priorities. Money, ministry, and position have replaced the old-time values of commitment and fidelity. Our time has been consumed with climbing the ladder of success, fame, and fortune. Often we have dressed those three longstanding prostitutes in religious garments and escorted them in and out of our churches and workplaces. We rationalize our behavior by saying that we're doing it for God—or maybe even for our families. But deep down we're committing spiritual adultery, which occasionally leads to physical adultery. We've left our first love.

It seems that many who speak of the necessity of revival in this generation have lost sight that there must be a revival of the priority of family life if there will ever be a general revival within society. Darkness in society often begins in the darkness of our own homes. When God led me to pastor the church in Germany, He worked deeply in my heart to rearrange my priorities. Through my son's illness and the new openness in communication with my wife, I came away from that time with clearly defined priorities for my life: God, first (my daily fellowship and relationship with Him, not my ministry); my family, second; and my ministry or work, third.

When I later returned to the United States to accept a call to be a pastor, I told the church of my priorities before I ever accepted the call. I told them frankly, "If I ever have to choose between adequate time with my family and adequate time with the church, I've already made the decision. I've chosen my family over the church. If I lose my work and ministry, I still can start over again and rebuild. But if I lose my family because of my wrong priorities, then I have lost much of my own credibility in ministry."

The churches where I ministered readily accepted those priorities in my life. It even caused them to reevaluate the entire church program in light of those three priorities. As a result, God built into us a life message that was able to penetrate the darkness in our community.

As a traveling evangelist during the past several years, I've had to work even more diligently to maintain those priorities. I've made a commitment to my family and the board of directors of our ministry to limit the number of days that I'm away from my family. Often I'm invited to speak to a large meeting, but I must decline because I'm at the limit established to protect my family times. It can become very tempting to violate those priorities. It would be easy to rationalize and say that I'm doing it for God. But I know that the battle for this generation will be won when we live by God's priorities for our lives, including nurturing our families.

Second, Christians struggle in their homes due to many of their past role models. The Christian church has a great heritage of men and women who impacted their generations for Christ. However, I am convinced that many of them would be forced to rearrange their priorities if they were ministering in the context of this generation. I know those words will knock over a few sacred cows, but we must understand that many warriors for Christ who fought valiantly for their generations had an understanding of marriage and family values that was occasionally below the biblical norm; indeed, their approach would be incapable of meeting the needs of *this* generation.

---

*Christians have tried to do battle
with eighteenth-century swords
and pistols while the enemy attacks
with twenty-first-century smart
bombs and laser beams.*

For instance, consider John Wesley, whose devotion to God has already been mentioned. He wrote in 1751, "I cannot understand how a Methodist preacher can answer it to God to preach one sermon or travel one day less, in a married than in a single state. In this respect surely 'it remaineth that they who have wives be as though they had none.'"[1] Wesley's contemporary, George Whitefield, had a similar attitude toward marriage. He stated, "I hope God will never suffer me to say, 'I have married a wife and therefore I cannot come.'"[2]

Both Whitefield and Wesley were mightily used of God. But it be would spiritual suicide for a Christian to adapt such a philosophy today.

Many of those who have entered into the battle today have studied the men of days gone by and their strategies to impact their generation. They have followed the examples of those great saints. Consequently, Christians have tried to do battle with eighteenth-century swords and pistols while the enemy attacks with twenty-first-century smart bombs and laser beams. Wesley and Whitefield were not lesser men of God because they didn't understand the great importance of the family in their generation. They didn't face some of the challenges to family values that we face at the close of the twentieth century. But anyone who attempts to copy their lifestyles today will find themselves in deep trouble.

Every generation of Christians must have a fresh visit from heaven and every generation of believers must fight in the context of the evil which plagues their contemporaries. Therefore, we must be careful to understand the nature of the battle and how it is to be fought at this important moment in history. The family is under an immense assault during these significant times.

Third, Christians struggle in their homes because they have not fully comprehended the cultural context of the battle. Technology and our culture, including pornography and questionable movie themes and television programs, have combined to threaten the family. When I traveled into Romania during the eighties, there were three questions always asked at the border: "Do you have any Bibles, any pornography, or any weapons?" All three were considered dangerous to Ceaucescu's evil regime. Actually, the communists were correct in their evaluation of their danger to their society. The Bible had the power to destroy the ideological foundation of communism. Pornography could dissolve the moral and family structure, while weapons could eradicate the military power of a dictatorial regime.

People often ask me about the dangers that I faced while traveling in a totalitarian state. Honestly, I have felt safer many times traveling into the darkest communist countries than traveling amidst the corruption that I constantly face in America. During the dark days of communism in Eastern Europe the enemy was easily recognizable. One needed only to stand firm in the truth of the Word of God. But in the West the attacks of Satan have been much more subtle. He doesn't come to us dressed as an evil dictator, but he comes arrayed in the cloak of wealth, beauty, and power. He speaks the language of Zion and calls himself our friend.

I once asked a businessman in the U.S. how he dealt with temptations he faced because of his heavy travel schedule. I knew that it must be very difficult on his family life. He said, "There's one thing that I purpose in my heart when I travel—I don't turn on the television set in the hotel room. I consider it Satan's instrument. I unplug it and leave it alone. I treat it like a snake." That may sound drastic to some, but I believe that he understood the great danger that has come to us in an age of transportation, communication, and entertainment.

Once, while traveling to a conference in Canada, I discussed this matter with a denominational leader who was also on the airplane. His comments were similar to those of the businessman. "I've seen Christian leaders who've been greatly used of God in their local communities. Then they begin to travel and speak about their victories. And they lose their power with God," he said. "They turn on a television set in the privacy of their rooms thinking that no one will know that they are watching obscene movies. But God knows, and they no longer have power in prayer. They stand in danger of allowing things into their minds and hearts that could destroy their family life as well as their effectiveness for God. Many such leaders have come to me for counsel."

Many hotels offer not only R-rated movies on pay per view but even X-rated movies. Such programming is now available on home cable too. We live in a cultural setting in the West that has increasingly become antagonistic toward Christianity. It can be partly attributed to the fact that the Christian church has lost her distinctiveness. We are quick to talk about family values, but often our standards in private are no different from those in the dark world around us. Behind the closed doors of many of our homes, there appears to be a character shortage. If the darkness in Western civilization is to be penetrated, the light must shine brightly in and through godly Christian homes.

The character of the Christian is the key issue in the battle for the family as well as society. Christlike character is the platform from which the assault on evil is launched. But someone might object, saying, "I'm trying to live for Christ, but no one else in my family is even interested in spiritual things. Does it mean that I'm losing the battle?"

Absolutely not! We cannot force anyone, including our own spouses and children, to accept the light of the gospel. But we can be a dwelling place for that light to shine brightly. They may never embrace the light, but they'll never be able to honestly deny that they have seen it. That's why the apostle Paul said that Christians were not to leave their spouses if they were unbelievers. Their only hope to accept the light is through the witness of the believing spouse (1 Corinthians 7:10–15). That does not necessarily mean that they will become followers of Jesus Christ. It simply implies that the only hope for their salvation and sanctification lies in the character of the believing spouse.

PROTECTING OUR MARRIAGES

Jerry Jenkins has written a very helpful book entitled *Loving Your Marriage Enough to Protect It*. In it Jenkins outlines some practical ways in which we can protect our marriages and homes. He says, the lack of "protective hedges that spouses should plant" around their marriages is a major cause of marital breakups in the Christian community. He goes on to list six practical hedges that he built around his marriage. He argues every married man and woman should determine their own, which may differ from his. Jenkins's list is shown below as an example of how he has learned to protect his own marriage.

1. Whenever I need to meet or dine or travel with an unrelated woman, I make it a threesome. Should an unavoidable last minute complication make this impossible, my wife hears it from me first.

2. I am careful about touching. While I might shake hands or squeeze a shoulder in greeting, I embrace only dear friends or relatives, and only in front of others.
3. If I pay a compliment, it is on clothes or hairstyles, not on the person herself. Commenting on a pretty outfit is much different, in my opinion, than telling a woman that she herself looks pretty.
4. I avoid flirtation or suggestive conversation, even in jest.
5. I remind my wife often—in writing or orally—that I remember my wedding vows: "Keeping you only unto me for as long as we both shall live."
6. From the time I get home from work until the children go to bed, I do no written or office work. This gives me lots of time with the family and for my wife and me to continue to court and date.[3]

FIVE HEDGES TO PROTECT US

It would be helpful for any Christian to follow Jenkins's advice in these dark days when the family is under tremendous attack. Whether one adopts these hedges or determines his or her own practical guidelines for protecting oneself and his family, it is imperative to build a wall of protection around our families. I would suggest that we not only build social hedges around our homes, but also spiritual ones, because the great arenas of battle take place in the human heart. Here are five hedges—character qualities that when present in our lives will serve to protect us from the assaults of Satan. But they will also help us in launching an attack against the forces of evil.

Humility

I list humility first because it is the one character quality upon which all of the others are built. Character is a work of grace in the human heart. In our own human strength it's impossible to make ourselves like Christ. It's only by God's grace that we are what we are and that we can reach the full potential that God desires for us. The Scriptures say, "God is opposed to the proud, but gives grace to the humble" (James 4:6, 1 Peter 5:5). It is out of a heart of humility that Christlike character is fashioned. The very nature of Christ is humility (Philippians 2:6–8). I am convinced that at the root of the fall of James, Carl, and Oscar lies the ancient sin of pride. As they began to experience a little success (in secular terms, not Christian ones), they began to compare themselves to others. They saw themselves in a higher position than others because of the numbers that they attracted to their churches and crusades. When we elevate ourselves in our own minds above others, we are headed for a tragic fall. Certainly, we cease to grow in Christlike character. And the first people likely to be affected by consequences of our arrogance will be our families.

Humility builds a wall of grace that protects the human heart. Pride provides a crack in that wall whereby the enemy is enabled to plunder, rob, and steal. Humility compares us to Christ while pride compares us to others. Humility is quick to say, "I'm wrong." Pride always says, "I'm right." Humility says, "I need you." Pride boasts, "I can do it myself." Humility decreases the self-life so that God can exalt us. Pride exalts self so that God has to reduce us. Humility builds a hedge around us. Pride opens the gates of hell against us.

Love

A friend once came to me for advice and said, "Sammy, I don't love my wife anymore. I just don't think that I can live with her." My advice to him was simply, "Love your wife. If you honestly don't have any feelings toward her, then confess it to God. Ask Him to fill you with His love. His grace is sufficient to restore those feelings that you once knew. But it first begins with a commitment to that relationship."

Love is the second hedge to protect us against Satan's assaults. Love isn't a funny feeling. It's commitment. Love involves emotions, but it's much more than that. It's a relationship rooted in grace and commitment. The Bible compares the love of a husband and wife to that of Christ and the church.

Early in my marriage, I began to meditate on how Christ loved the church. During that time God helped me to understand how I am to love my wife. That understanding has helped me to build a wall of protection around our family. Christ's love for the church is fresh every day. The church has been in existence for close to 2,000 years, and His love never grows old. As I began to understand the nature of His love, I saw how I had begun to take my wife for granted. God gave me a deep conviction that I needed to thank Him every day for putting her into my life as well as express regularly my appreciation to her.

Christ loved the church until the end. I'm so thankful that He didn't climb halfway up Mt. Calvary and say, "This is too tough. I can't go through with it. I loved the church 95 percent of the way. But I just can't handle the last 5 percent." Christ committed Himself to the end. That's the love commitment He calls us to: "Until death do us part." If our families are to survive during these perilous times, then we must have an unflinching commitment to our relationship. That commitment will lead us through dark and difficult days even as Christ's love gives us the strength to face the worst of circumstances. In any marriage there will be times when we feel like throwing in the towel. Those are the times in which true love is tested, and we must remember the commitment that we have made to one another.

Christ loved us especially when we were wrong and rebellious. The amazing part of His love for us is that He did not love us because we first loved Him. He loved us even when we rebelled against Him. I find it easy to love my wife and children when they agree with me. But the real test of Christlike love comes when I love them when we disagree—or when they have wronged me. Christ's love cries from the cross, "Forgive them!" Christ's love can only be understood in terms of grace. Grace is what God has done for us even though we don't deserve it. And grace is that which builds character into our lives. Forgiveness is one of the greatest needs in the family unit today. A family unable to forgive will find the fiery darts of guilt and bitterness hurled at them from the enemy. But the family rooted in the grace that flows from the cross will know an inpenetrable hedge of love surrounding them.

Openness

I was devastated by a pastor whom I trusted, admired, and loved. He left his wife for another woman. When I sat down to discuss what happened he said to me, "Ten years ago we quit communicating with one another. What you are seeing in our lives now is simply the lack of intimate interaction over a long period of time." Although that was no excuse for his actions, I believe that he was probably right. I've seen the same thing happen numerous times. A young couple is deeply in love. Somewhere along the way one or both of them are hurt by the other. Then they begin to close up and quit communicating. Transparency and truthfulness will open the heart so that restoration can occur. But silence and secrets tear down the hedge of protection around the family.

Openness is crucial to protect our families and strengthen us for spiritual battles. The essence of the life of Christ can be described by transparent communication. A primary purpose in Christ's visit to this earth was to reveal openly to all men the very nature and character of God. If anyone wants to know what God is like, he can look to the Son. God didn't keep His eternal attributes a secret from us. But He in His infinite love for us honestly exposed Himself to us. "He is the radiance of His glory and the exact representation of His nature" (Hebrews 1:3).

In becoming like Christ we must learn to be open and honest with one another. Love must grow, or it becomes stagnant and stale. And love can only grow in an atmosphere of transparency and truthfulness.

Respect

There's been much talk in recent years about the wife's responsibility to submit to her husband. However, the apostle Paul spoke of mutual submission before he ever mentioned the wife's duty. He said, "And be subject to one another in the fear [reverence] of Christ" (Ephesians 5:21). It's extremely important that an attitude of respect for each other be maintained in the family unit. It will lead to a healthy respect for the dignity of every family member.

One of the deepest needs of the human heart is for a sense of significance. God has placed great value on human life—so much that He sent Christ to die on a cruel Roman cross to save us from eternal damnation. Only God's love can enable us to understand how really valuable we are. But the expression of that love is most clearly seen in the context of the family. That's why I've occasionally gotten off an airplane (coming from some far away country) and have rushed to a basketball game in which my son or daughter has been playing. With bloodshot eyes from the lack of sleep, I've shouted and cheered for them. I knew how important it has been for them to know that they are valuable and what they do is significant. I really believe that it was just as spiritual to cheer at that game as it was to preach the crusade. Both were an expression of God's love.

Mutual respect produces healthy hearts and healthy homes. The family becomes a haven of safety in times of Satan's assault.

Faithfulness

Jeremiah and the great hymn writer both exclaimed, "Great is Thy faithfulness!" Throughout the ages the faithfulness of God has proven true over and over again. Even when the church has been faithless, God remained faithful to His word and His people. As I look back over twenty-five years of marriage and ministry, I am overwhelmed with the faithfulness of God. There have been times when God had every right to give up on me. But He didn't. His love continued and lifted me up when I had fallen.

His faithfulness becomes an example of what He desires for me and my family to know and experience. The spirit of the age is one in which loyalty and faithfulness seem antiquated. And that's why marriages are falling apart. The Christian must have a deep commitment to developing a faithful heart and life. The lure of Satan will always be around the corner, at the office, or maybe even at church. Therefore, the Christian must determine in his heart to keep his eyes, hands, and heart only for his spouse.

There are three practical principles that have helped me to develop and maintain loyalty and faithfulness to my wife. First, I refuse to share any of the intimate desires, dreams, and needs of my life with any other woman. Second, I make every attempt not to allow myself to get into unhealthy situations that could lead to a lack of faithfulness. Third, I have made a commitment not to watch movies, read publications, or participate in any form of entertainment that would cause me to fantasize about other women. Faithfulness may be labeled as outdated in Western civilization, but it's certainly one of the great attributes of God. When we allow Him to build this characteristic into our lives, we discover that His faithfulness is great—great enough to protect our marriage.

Western civilization is on the fast track to self-destruction. Moral devastation and spiritual ruin will quickly devour the very fabric of society unless there is immediate treatment. I believe that God's prescription begins with the family, and in particular the Christian family. He has issued a call for soldiers on the battlefield of life. But there are two items of business for those who have enlisted. First, get your priorities straight. Second, commit yourself to developing and growing in Christlike character in relationship to your family.

A great many delight to read about the spiritual life, but that is not enough. I must buy. At what price? Give up all. You must sell all to buy the pearl of great price. Come with every sin and every folly, all temper, everything you love, your whole life, and place it in the possession of Christ. Die to everything and be fully given up to God. It is only in the vessel that is fully cleansed that the Holy Spirit can do His work.

Andrew Murray
The Spiritual Life

If we confess our sins, He is faithful and righteous to forgive us our sins and to cleanse us from all unrighteousness.

1 John 1:9

6

The Wounded Soldier

It had been almost fifteen years since I had sat down face-to-face for a talk with my friend. Seeing Randall (not his real name) again was probably one of the most awkward, difficult moments of my ministry. My hands were sweaty and my heart was racing. I knew that God had orchestrated the meeting, but I surely wasn't looking forward to it. I came to spend time in prayer with my pastor friend, and there I also found Randall sitting in his office.

Actually, I had come not only to pray with my pastor friend, but also to tell him that I wouldn't be able to lead a citywide prayer gathering. The reason was Randall, pastor of one of the largest churches in the city. Fifteen years earlier, when Randall had been my pastor, we had sat down for a heart-to-heart talk. A young person told me that she had accidently come upon Randall and the church secretary romantically embracing one another. I didn't want to believe it. I told the youth that she was on dangerous ground, accusing God's anointed like that. I had no other choice but to ask Randall about the incident.

I asked a close friend to go with me. Together we asked Randall and the secretary to meet with us. I told them what had been communicated to me. "I just need to hear from you that it's not true. I'll go back to that teenager," I said, "and tell her not to continue to spread such rumors."

"It is true, Sammy. We love one another."

My heart broke. I wanted to cry, to shout, to run away. I had moved to the city at Randall's encouragement. His church would be an anchor, its members praying for us as we conducted our international ministry. Furthermore, Randall was a great Bible teacher and a great man of prayer; he had been such an encouragement to me. *How could he do this?* I begged him to repent.

"We've tried to repent. We've asked God to take these feelings away from us, but He hasn't. We deeply love one another. But I really don't have time to talk about it right now. I have to teach a Bible study," he calmly told me.

I couldn't believe it! I was almost as shocked by his nonchalant attitude toward our conversation as I was by his sin. I told my colleague, "If someone had confronted me with such a sin, I would be devastated. There's no way that I could go and teach a Bible study after that."

I knew what I needed to do. With fear and trembling I approached the leaders of the church and informed them of what had transpired. A meeting was set for that evening. Randall, his wife, my colleague, the leaders, and I all met in the most somber of settings.

Randall refused to budge and remained unrepentant. "You know what this means," one of the leaders told him. "We'll have to inform the church about this."

"I know," he said quietly.

The leaders all silently left the church. Tex and I sat up most of the night talking about what had happened—and reevaluating our own marriage.

We were surprised the next morning when Randall showed up at our front door. With tears streaming down his face he cried out, "It's over, Sammy! It's over! I've repented, and it's over." We both fell on our faces and soaked my living room floor with tears as we prayed, wept, and rejoiced.

At the Wednesday evening worship service, Randall stood and confessed his sin to the church. The secretary resigned her position at the church and said that the relationship with Randall was over. The church in an act of love committed themselves to help restore Randall to his fellowship with God, his family, and his position of leadership. It was one of those stories that seemed to have a great ending.

Not long after that I left to travel in some evangelistic endeavors. When I returned to my home, I discovered that Randall had resigned the church and left his wife. Shortly afterward he married the secretary.

That was the last time I had spoken with him in depth. Over the years I had seen him in a restaurant or at a minister's gathering. But we had never sat down for an in-depth talk since that last meeting with the church leaders. Randall soon became associate pastor of a church that had just been started by a pastor in a similar situation to his. This pastor, whom I'll call Alan, had also left his wife and children, married another woman, and began the new church. The church grew rapidly.

Eventually Randall left that church and began one on his own. Both churches became two of the largest in the city, having thousands in attendance.

Years passed. Everyone seemed to let bygones be bygones. Both men were looked upon with prestige within the Christian community. Randall served as pastor chairman of the National Day of Prayer for our city. Both pastors were always asked to assume leadership roles in any large citywide gathering. That's why I struggled that day when I walked into the office of my pastor friend. I had agreed to lead the citywide prayer assembly. But I didn't know that it was scheduled to be held in the large church begun by Randall's colleague who had also left his wife.

GRACE VERSUS JUDGMENT

So there I was, feeling tremendous emotional and spiritual conflict. What should my attitude be toward Randall and Alan? Should it be one of complete grace and forgiveness? Or should I stand firm on the biblical standard that those men had relinquished their position of leadership within the body of Christ when they left their wives? If I took such a stand would I be kicking wounded soldiers? Or would I be compromising my convictions by recognizing their leadership if I agreed to guide the citywide prayer gathering? The tension between God's standard of holiness and His gift of grace seemed to be pulling me in two separate directions.

Before I could answer those questions, I needed to know that my decision would honor Christ above all else. During our meeting in his office Alan told me, "I believe God has raised me up and given me this leadership position. I didn't open the door. God has opened it for me. My ministry has grown, and He has done it." He implied that I would be actually judging God if I didn't agree to lead the prayer gathering.

I excused myself and returned home to ponder his comments. *Was I to trust the circumstances or to follow the guidelines of God's Word?* I had to decide whether I could trust this pastor's experience—his rise and recognition in the city as a spiritual leader. Or should I trust the biblical standard (1 Timothy 3) as the basis of spiritual leadership? After two days of prayer and heart searching, I knew that I must trust the Bible as my final authority on such matters. As I prayed through the circumstances and studied the Scriptures, I came to some very definite conclusions.

Ultimately, my decision was determined by principles found in the Bible. I believe that our attitudes toward such issues will affect potential revival in America. We can become judgmental on one hand, and God will never bless that kind of spirit. On the other hand, we can do great damage to the name, honor, and kingdom of Christ if there is not biblical accountability for those in leadership.

In reaching my decision whether to support the prayer conference under this pastor's leadership, I first had to know my appropriate response to the pastor. This required my dealing with two separate but related issues. First, I needed to know how to help restore a person to his personal fellowship with

God. Second, I needed to know how and when to help restore a person back to his place of spiritual leadership. The distinction between the two is significant and needs to be dealt with on two different levels.

For example, a pastor friend came to me one day and told me that he was going to have a particular pastor speak in his church. The invited speaker once had a sexual tryst with a woman in the congregation where he pastored. The church eventually found out about it and released him even though he confessed his sin and stated his repentance. He was left out in the streets, with no job and a shattered marriage. My pastor friend said what I've heard since, "Sometimes Christians are the only ones who shoot their wounded. I believe in the principle of restoration and that we need to help this man. We need to let him know that we care about him and are willing to stand with him."

"I agree that we ought to do everything to help restore him," I said. "But restore him to what? Fellowship with God or to a leadership position in ministry? Or both? What is that we really want to do?" I asked.

Then I encouraged my pastor friend. "Let's help this man. It's been my experience that when a man has an affair like this, it's normally not a one-time failure. I believe that there are probably some deep issues in his life that must be dealt with before he is placed before the people speaking the Word of God. Also, he and his wife are going to need time to deal with the hurt that has been inflicted upon them by this sin."

"Why don't you ask the pastor to become a part of your church? Help him to find a job. Take him under your wing for a year, and help him deal with the deep issues in his heart. When the credibility of his character is restored, then let him speak in the church," I said.

"Sammy," the pastor responded, "I believe God's forgiveness is instantaneous. He removes our sins as far as the east is from the west when He pardons us. Therefore, I believe that we ought to give him a chance right now."

"I understand what you are saying," I argued, "but I believe that it will be spiritual suicide to put this man so quickly back into the battle. When a soldier is wounded in warfare, he is taken to the hospital immediately for treatment and rehabilitation. Those in charge would never send a wounded soldier back into battle. That's not a lack of concern or grace. It's just the opposite. It's grace and concern that places the wounded soldier somewhere far away from the intensity of the battle so that healing can be applied to the wounds. When the soldier is fully restored to spiritual health and stability, only then is he capable to reenter the center of the raging conflict."

My pastor friend disagreed, however. He asked the fallen pastor to speak in his church. A few months later he fell again into immorality. It broke my heart. Possibly the tragedy could have been avoided. Now restoration for the fallen pastor would be that much more difficult. But even more than that, the name of Christ had been dishonored. Sometimes the church is so concerned with restoring wounded soldiers to the battle that we forget they need healing and rehabilitation first. As a result, great damage can be done in the kingdom of God.

Thus far we have considered the nature of the battle and qualities for being an effective soldier. But what happens when the soldier is wounded? Beyond his pain—and ours—over the loss, is there any hope for his returning to the battle? Can he help the battle for the kingdom of God? That final question is the most important one.

A pastor once told me that he was dealing with a situation involving a well-known Christian leader whose sin had become public. He said that several people called him saying, "We've got to save this man's ministry." But no one called him and expressed a concern for the impact upon the kingdom of God. Our greatest concern must be God's kingdom. That includes concern for all parties involved in the tragedy of sin as well as refusing to compromise the honor and name of Christ among God's people.

Yes, we can restore our wounded soldiers to the battlefield. Let me offer three principles in restoring wounded soldiers. By *wounded soldiers* I mean those that have been injured by an act of their own will—those who have violated the Commander's orders while in battle. I'm not speaking of those who have been injured by hurts inflicted upon them by others. Their response to those injuries could be included in these principles. Often such hurts are wrongly inflicted, and I caution them not to to wallow in false guilt caused by wrongful condemnations. But for our purposes here I am speaking of soldiers who have been wounded by their own violation of God's standard.

No Compromise

First, we must adhere to the standard of God. We cannot compromise; we cannot call sin by any other name. We must raise high the banner of holiness. We'll never understand the beauty of God's grace until we've come face-to-face with His holiness. The great hymns of the faith consistently give witness to this great truth. John Newton wrote, "Amazing grace, how sweet the sound, that saved a wretch like me." When we see God in all His splendor and purity, we fall before Him with a deep sense of our own wretchedness. That sense of anguish drives us to call unto Him for grace. His pardon is then applied to our wounded hearts.

One reason Eastern European Christians have seen God work in such a marvelous manner is because they have refused to compromise the standard of God. But the missing word in evangelical preaching and ministry in the West today is *repentance*. Yet it's the hallmark of believers in Eastern Europe. They were known during the dismal days of communism as *repenters*. Their call to salvation has been a call to repent and trust Christ.

Repentance is a basic change of heart and mind. When a Christian sins, a deep wound is inflicted upon his heart. The healing ointment of grace cannot be applied to that wound until there has been a change of attitude about the cause of the wound. That turning normally takes place as we behold God's holiness. His absolute purity causes us to see the cross in a new and intimate way. We begin to understand that particular sin was the reason that Jesus died 2,000 years ago. When we comprehend the horror of our sin, the result is deep repentance. It's not simply sorrow for what we've done wrong or because we've been caught in our transgression. It's getting honest with God and ourselves. It's forsaking our attitude or action that crucified the Savior.

His Healing Grace

That brings us to the second principle. We must apply grace to the hurting heart. The standard of God, His law, acts as a tutor that clearly explains the purpose of Christ's death on the cross. It instructs us to come and prostrate ourselves at the foot of the cross. There we find God's grace; at the cross grace and mercy drop from the hands and side of Christ to the heart of the Christian. As the wounded soldier experiences God's love, supernatural healing begins to take place in his heart. When God says "Forgiven," He really means that we're forgiven.

Many Christians have a difficult time forgiving themselves as well as forgiving others. They need only to stay near the cross daily and allow that wonderful ointment of grace to be applied to the wounds.

God's grace acts as the miraculous medication that brings healing to the wounded warrior. Many Christians have a difficult time forgiving themselves as well as forgiving others. They need only to stay near the cross daily and allow that wonderful ointment of grace to be applied to the wounds. We must trust God that He has truly removed the cancer. We don't have to live in guilt and fear. God's grace acts as a cleansing agent that keeps the deadly infection of sin from destroying our lives.

There must be the balance of God's standard (the law) and God's grace. If we only apply God's standard to the wounded warrior, we leave him on the surgical bed with very little hope of recovery. But if we only apply the ointment of God's grace to the outward symptoms of his cancerous sin, it's only a matter of time before tragedy takes its toll on his life. Christians in the East and West could learn from one another how to apply this balance to their lives and churches.

The suffering in Eastern Europe mandated a strong call for repentance. Christians could not afford to have spiritual spies in their ranks. They were quick to look for the fruit of repentance among converts. However, in this new day of freedom, they've had much difficulty in adapting to the new situation and applying the grace of God to it. Many intellectuals and young people have had a difficult time being integrated into the church as older Christians became suspicious, even as the apostles were of the new convert Saul.

One Sunday morning in April 1993 I preached in the Baptist church of Norislk, Siberia, after a crusade in the city. Before the crusade, the church consisted of only a handful of elderly people. It was a joy for me to see the church packed with teens and young adults who came to know Christ through our ministry. The entire youth choir singing that morning had been converted during the crusade. But after the service one of the leaders expressed his concern to me. "Sammy," he said, "the elderly people who survived the persecution are afraid of all these new young people in the church. They have suffered much and have stood uncompromisingly for Christ. But sometimes they put such extreme demands on them, I'm afraid that we may lose some of them."

If surgery is performed by the standard of God's holiness but there's not the application of God's grace to the wounds of the believer, the results will be a spiritual infection that can quickly spread doing immense damage to the body of Christ. Eastern European Christians can learn from believers in the West about the application of God's grace. And Western Christians can learn from Eastern European believers to lift high the standard of God's holiness. We can learn spiritual balance from one another. Such balance will produce stable and healthy soldiers in the battle.

Taking Time

But there's a third principle for restoring wounded soldiers: we must grant the wounded warrior *time*. Surgery can be accomplished on one occasion. Grace can be applied immediately from the healing waters that flow freely from the fountain of the cross. However, it still takes time for the wounds to heal. Some wounds will take longer than others to heal. It depends upon how deep the wounds are and how dangerous the infection is to the body. As a person lives close to the cross, grace and mercy are consistently applied to the wounds. Over a period of time the wounds heal and become scars that fade from the body as the months and years pass.

Here are two considerations for Christians as they attempt to restore a wounded soldier. First, we must be confident of their spiritual health before placing them into the forefront of the conflict. Second, their credibility must be fully restored before they can reenter the battle in a position of leadership. I have seen well-intentioned Christians do great harm to the body of Christ by placing a wounded soldier back into the heat of the battle before there has been sufficient healing of his hurts.

There's one aspect of spiritual warfare that we must always remember: Satan will make every attempt to attack the soldier at the place of his wound. When he sees spiritual bandages wrapped around a soldier, he will immediately attack at that point, attempting to unravel them. That's why Paul says that a leader in the battle should not be a new convert "lest he become conceited and fall into the condemnation incurred by the devil" (1 Timothy 3:6). The great danger is that a wounded soldier can easily forget that he has wounds in the heat of the battle. He becomes overconfident and arrogant. Satan then attacks him at the point of his wound, and he finds himself in need of spiritual surgery again. Meanwhile, the battle continues to rage while the soldier has to spend even more time in recovery.

But how does one know when he's ready again for the heat of the battle? I believe that other Christians will be more able than himself to confirm that the healing process has been sufficiently completed. That's why close relationships within the church are vital. One of the best things a wounded soldier can do is submit himself to a small accountability or discipleship group that will love and nurse him back to recovery and spiritual health. The members will be able to help him find his place in the battle again.

THE CREDIBILITY OF A LEADER

Christians must be especially careful in dealing with leaders who have fallen. Paul not only stated that a leader must have a certain level of spiritual maturity, but he must also have credibility within and without the church. He says, "And he must have a good reputation with those outside the church, so that he may not fall into reproach and the snare of the devil" (1 Timothy 3:7). It's interesting that in cases of both immaturity (verse 6) and a lack of credibility (verse 7) Paul says Satan has a great opportunity to hinder the effectiveness of the church. We are called to do battle with the devil. Therefore we must give him no opportunity to back us into a corner where we remain continually in a defensive position rather than an offensive one.

Paul said that leaders must have credibility for two reasons: (1) "the snare of the devil," and (2) "the reproach of the devil." The snare of the devil does tremendous damage to the soldier himself. But the reproach of the devil does great harm to the honor and name of Christ and His kingdom. That's one major reason why the church in the West today finds herself on the defensive rather than the offensive. That's why we find ourselves defending ourselves more than we are proclaiming the gospel.

During the recent trip to Siberia, I was forced to spend three days and two nights in one of the domestic airports in Moscow because of a fuel shortage. Airline officials kept promising that the flights would leave in two or three hours. That went on for three days. Hundreds of people were trapped, tired, and frustrated. During that time my interpreter, Vladimir, said to me, "Sammy, there are people here just like there are in Siberia. We're the only ones in the airport with good news. Let's hold a crusade in the airport. Let's preach the gospel here."

I must be honest. I was skeptical. How would people respond to an American evangelist taking advantage of such a situation? But Vladimir insisted. "Come on, Sammy, let's go preach." I hesitantly went with him.

I stood among the hundreds of weary travelers and told them that I too was exhausted from waiting for two days and having to sleep on the floor. I said, "But I have some very good news for you this evening." I then began to preach the gospel message. To my surprise people listened attentively. More began to gather around eager to hear the message. At the close of the message, Vladimir said, "Give an invitation for people to come to Christ, Sammy."

"Now. Here?" I responded.

"Yes. Now! Here!" he said.

As I extended the invitation for people to repent of sins and place their faith in Christ, I was shocked when sixty people got out of their seats and came to where I was standing and prayed with me. Many of them with tears running down their faces invited Christ into their lives. It was a beautiful and unusual moment for me.

After we finished counseling them, I was lying on my suitcase thinking, "What would have happened if this were Chicago's O'Hare or London's Heathrow Airport?" Perhaps it was my little faith, but I concluded that the response of the people would have been entirely different. There's a completely different spiritual atmosphere in Eastern Europe than in North America and Western Europe. It's one that's conducive for a spiritual harvest. I believe that atmosphere has been created partially by the credibility factor. When I stood in that Moscow airport and preached the gospel, I was immediately standing on the platform of credibility. In Chicago or London I would have somehow had to build that platform before I could have seen such results.

RANDALL AND THE PRAYER CONFERENCE

That's why I made the decision not to lead the citywide prayer conference. Randall and his colleague, Alan, lost their ability to lead when they left their wives because they lost their credibility. Because the decision they made would be one on public record for the rest of their lives, they no longer had the credibility to speak of the victory that Jesus can give in the marital relationship. One of my neighbors attended Randall's large church. He had an affair with another woman, but Randall could not credibly tell him that Jesus could give him victory over that relationship. Randall made a decision that would follow him the rest of his life. That doesn't mean that he could never be forgiven or that he could never minister again. It simply means that his unrepentance had eliminated him from leadership within the Christian community.

The qualification for leadership doesn't consist of how large a congregation one has, or how well he can teach the Word of God. Actually, Paul lists the qualifications for spiritual leadership in 1 Timothy 3. Those qualifications can be divided into three different categories: (1) godly character, which is mentioned most; (2) family life and relationships, which are the second most mentioned category; (3) abilities, which are mentioned least. We in the West have many times elevated ones into leadership with great abilities to preach, teach, and organize, but take little care of their personal and family lives. Our true spiritual ability to minister should be an outgrowth of our walk with God and our families. Let's face the truth. We don't have the ability to pierce the darkness in this generation because much of the time we are just as defeated as the world around us.

---

*Restoration to complete fellowship
with God should be the goal
for every wounded soldier.*

So, just what should happen to men and women who have fallen like Randall? First, there must be deep repentance in their hearts. Second, they need to go to the cross to receive grace and find healing for their wounded hearts. These two principles will bring full restoration to their fellowship with God. Third, they need to submit themselves to a group who loves them and will nurture them back to health. They need to be accountable to that group and return to the furor of the battle only when they can agree that they are prepared spiritually for the battle. Fourth, if they occupy a leadership position in the Christian community, and have committed sin that places them in reproach of the community, they should withdraw from leadership until their credibility has been reestablished. If they are unable to fully restore and rectify that situation, they should humbly withdraw from their position of leadership.

To some that may seem harsh. However, if the church in the West is ever to see a great revival, we must once again become believable. We are quick to point our fingers at the abortionists and homosexuals. But many of them laugh and sneer at us because they say, "They're just like us." In order for revival to come to the West, we must come to grips with the grave consequences of sin in the life of the church.

The platform of credibility must be rebuilt. Certainly, Randall's sin is not unforgivable. And he can have limited ministry to others. But he and others who, because of their sin, have lost their ability to restore relationships with their fellow man must realize that they have lost their credibility. They should be willing to humbly remove themselves from leadership in the body of Christ in order that they don't give Satan any opportunity to dishonor the name of Christ. Such an act would in itself begin to make the Christian church once again believable.

Restoration to complete fellowship with God should be the goal for every wounded soldier. The Christian community should do everything possible to help restore them to their intimacy with God and to the front lines of the battlefield. Every believer is needed in the battle. We must also determine to rebuild the platform of credibility from which the attack against the forces of evil is launched. The place of leadership must be reserved for those who have been willing to build and lead from the platform of credibility. Only then will we be capable of building an army that can shatter the darkness.

Part 3
The Weapons of Warfare

He will lead you on the field with courage, and bring you off with honor. He lived and died for you; He will live and die with you. His mercy and tenderness to His soldiers are unmatched.

William Gurnall
The Christian in Complete Armour

Put on the full armor of God, that you may be able to stand firm against the schemes of the devil.

Ephesians 6:11

7

The Soldier's Defense

Leningrad, U.S.S.R.; Easter 1974: "You cannot do this. It is illegal in the Soviet Union," shouted the interrogator. "We believe religion is the opiate of the people. You have spread your opiate among the masses of the Soviet people. This is a crime against our state."

Fred and I sat quietly listening to the interrogator angrily denounce Christianity and accuse us. We were caught speaking to university students about our faith in Jesus Christ. After eight hours of interrogation, the agent said, "By the year 2000 Christianity will no longer exist! There are only old people in the church. By then they will have died and communism will have won a great victory over the myth of Christianity."

Krasnoyarsk, Siberia; July 1992: I recalled the Soviet agent's words tonight. Thousands of Siberians had filled the stadium to hear a message of hope. God led me to preach on the second coming of Christ. During my message, I told about what happened to me in Leningrad. I recounted the words of our interrogator. "Well, it's 1992. The Soviet Union no longer exists and Christianity is advancing with tens of thousands of Russians turning to faith in Christ."

The crowd broke into loud applause. For those Russians hungrily seeking after God, it was a moving moment. They were overwhelmed to realize that their government's constant attempts to wipe Christianity out of Russia had finally failed. Many wept as they pondered the greatness of God and the spiritual victory that Russian Christians had won. I have thought many times about the words of the interrogator, and it really is amazing—almost unbelievable—how God brought the church through a systematic attempt by Satan to destroy Christianity—not only in the Soviet Union, but throughout Eastern Europe.

In Romania, for instance, the Ceaucescu regime attempted to keep the Bible out of the country. Indeed, the day before one of our entries, border guards destroyed a van attempting to enter Romania; the guards had found Bibles hidden in the vehicle and literally tore it to pieces. On another occasion when guards discovered a large shipment of Bibles, Ceaucescu ordered that the Bibles be used as toilet paper. In Russia, Christians were not allowed to be educated. Children were not allowed to be taught the Scriptures, even in the churches.

Before the church begins to attack the strongholds of Satan, we must have a well fortified defensive position. It's a place of safety.

In East Germany, young people were forced to either join the Free German Youth (Communist Youth Organization) or the church. If they chose the church they faced enormous difficulties. A pastor friend of mine in Romania moved every night for six months from house to house in order not to be found by the Securitate.

With all of the attempts to destroy Christianity in Eastern Europe, how could the church survive and even grow during those difficult times? Christians had virtually no earthly power or authority. They were treated as the scum of the earth. In some places in Siberia, officials told the population that Baptists and Pentecostals offered their children as human sacrifices. Seemingly everything in their culture opposed them. How could they have blossomed under such oppression?

They understood that they were soldiers in God's army and had heavenly armor and spiritual weapons with which no government could contend. Throughout the ages evil dictators and corrupt governments have attempted to silence the voice of simple, humble believers in Jesus, the Christ. But no government or leader is capable of coping with the protective armor of God and the powerful spiritual weapons given to His people.

If the church in the West is not only to survive, but also grow during these dark days, then we must know our spiritual armor and the weapons of our warfare. The purpose of our armor is defensive—that which protects the church. The weapons of warfare (discussed in the next chapter) enable us to go on the offense against the forces of evil. However, before the church begins to attack the strongholds of Satan, we must have a well fortified defensive position. It's a place of safety. Without that strong defensive position, we will never be able to penetrate the enemy's territory. The Christian's defensive position lies in his knowledge of God, the enemy, and himself. Through this understanding he will know how to withstand the onslaught of Satan.

Know Your God

The greatest defense that the Christian has against Satan is a deep, intimate knowledge of God. Our victory doesn't depend on our strength and abilities, but in God Himself. He is our shield and defender. And "if God is for us, who is against us?" (Romans 8:31). One of the great declarations of God's protection for us appears in Psalm 91:1–4: "He who dwells in the shelter of the Most High will abide in the shadow of the Almighty. I will say to the Lord, 'My refuge and my fortress, my God in whom I trust!' For it is He who delivers you from the snare of the trapper, and from the deadly pestilence. He will cover you with His pinions, and under His wings you may seek refuge; His faithfulness is a shield and bulwark." God promises to be to us: a refuge, a fortress, our deliverer, our covering, a shield, and a bulwark. What more protection do we need? He is all that we need.

Many Christians who talk about spiritual warfare always talk about the devil. It is important to understand who he is and the ways in which he works. However, our primary emphasis should always be getting to know God, not the devil. In this very personal knowledge of God, we will find all of the protection that we will ever need. Three men I've met remain shining examples of believers who know their God and are able to withstand the flaming arrows of Satan.

In 1987 in Bratislava, Czechoslovakia, I approached a gentleman glowing with joy and peace. He had spent five years in prison for his faith. Though officials still banned him from any public ministry, privately he continued to serve the Lord. He walked me to the window of his apartment and pointed to the soccer stadium across the street and said, "Young man, every week that stadium is filled with people cheering for their favorite football team. One day it will be filled with people hearing the gospel of Jesus Christ."

To be honest, I thought to myself, *Old man, I don't think so —not in my lifetime, and for sure not in yours.* As I looked at the circumstances in the country, it seemed impossible. But he wasn't looking at the situation. His eyes were fixed on God. He knew God in a depth with which I still long to know Him.

In 1991 in Beijing, China, I nervously awaited a meeting. It hadn't been very long since the Tiananmen Square uprising had been crushed. But that dear Chinese Christian insisted on meeting me at the hotel. He came to my room and spoke openly, "I'm an old man now. What can they do to me? I've spent more than a decade in prison. God sustained me then and He will now. I don't fear what man can do. God is my place of safety. I lead a house church. It's growing. The gospel is spreading rapidly. Pray for us. We only need God. Pray that we will get to know Him."

I was overwhelmed. He knew God in ways far beyond what I knew. Yet his one desire was to know Him better.

Two years later in Kishinev, Moldavia, once again I watched an elderly gentleman whom I had seen many times before. He moved slowly, but always he was seated close to the pulpit. There seemed to be a constant smile on his face and a sparkle in his eyes. Something special warmed his countenance.

One of the English speaking ladies in the church asked me, "Sammy, do you know our oldest pastor?" Then she introduced me to the saintly gentleman. After being introduced, he began to tell of how he was imprisoned under Stalin's regime. He didn't speak of the many years of service in Christ's kingdom. But he spoke of the goodness and faithfulness of God through the years. He spoke of the friendship of God during years of oppression and the love of God during the new days of freedom. As he spoke, I smelled a fragrance in the room, the fragrance of the sweetness of a man who knew God.

In all three places—Czechoslovakia, China, and Moldavia —these men had determined to know God. Their objective in life didn't consist of big budgets and large crowds. Their one purpose was to know Him—just know Him. The gates of hell could not stand against men who knew Him so intimately. Perhaps that's why Paul wrote, "More than that, I count all things to be loss in view of the surpassing value of knowing Christ Jesus, my Lord, for whom I have suffered the loss of all things, and count them but rubbish in order that I may gain Christ . . . that I may know Him, and the power of His resurrection and the fellowship of His sufferings, being conformed unto His death" (Philippians 3:8, 10).

As the evil mounts in the West, we need men and women who really know God. They will be able to stand firm no matter how fierce the battle. When Paul wrote to the Ephesian Christians about the raging battle, he didn't tell them to go chasing after the devil. He said three times, "Stand firm" (Ephesians 6:11, 13–14). The believer simply needs to get to know God and stand in Him. As I have studied that Ephesians passage, I am always encouraged to remember the true nature of my spiritual armor and protection. Paul lists five pieces of armor: truth, righteousness, the gospel of peace, faith, and salvation. All of these pieces could be summed up in one word: *Jesus*. In actuality Paul was telling the believer to clothe himself daily with the knowledge of Christ. Dress yourself in the knowledge of Christ's truth and personal righteousness. Look to Him as the author and perfecter of your faith and the source of your peace. Place the protection of His salvation on your head, and the enemy will not be able to harm you. Get to know Him!

KNOW YOUR ENEMY

Several years ago I listened to an evangelist whom I respected greatly. He told of how he had been captive to many dark and evil desires of his heart—even while holding evangelistic crusades. He spoke of his bondage to immoral lusts as well as a gluttonous appetite. He wept as he spoke. Then he told how he had demons cast out of him. The more he spoke, the more intrigued I became. So, I jumped at the opportunity for my wife and I to have lunch with him and his wife.

When we made our order at the restaurant, I couldn't believe what I heard. He ordered three meals—one for his wife and two for himself. I thought to myself, *You can have multitudes of demons of gluttony cast out of you, but you will never have victory over gluttony until you have learned to crucify your flesh.* My colleague had wrongly identified the enemy by a narrow and imbalanced view of him and his ways.

The Christian must contend with three areas of attack: the battle within (with the flesh), the battle without (with the world), and the battle above (with the devil). One of the great problems with the church in the West is the tendency to emphasize one aspect of battle over another. Consequently, often we are left defenseless against the enemy.

For instance, during the Gulf War in 1991, the allied forces leaked information through the media to the Iraqis. They subtly stated that Kuwait City would be liberated by an invasion of marines on the beach. The occupying Iraqis prepared to defend the city. They placed their ground forces on the beach. If the allies attempted to take Kuwait City, they would face devastation—so they thought. With all their firepower placed at one location, they were taken by surprise when the allies chose not to storm the beach. Instead, the allies pulled a flank maneuver and sent troops around the city and entered through the desert. They captured Kuwait City with very little resistance.

Many Christians haven't understood the subtle ways of Satan. He's a master of deception and misinformation. We, like the Iraqis, buy into his misinformation and find ourselves defenseless. He attacks from an entirely different position. We must be prepared on every front.

James identifies all three areas of attack in chapter 3: the conflict within your members, verses 1–3; the conflict with the world system, verses 4–5; and the conflict with the devil, verses 6–8. The victorious Christian will understand all three areas of battle and prepare himself on every front. The reason the evangelist didn't have victory over gluttony was because he placed all his focus on the conflict with the devil and was totally unprepared for the conflict within his own members—what the Bible commonly calls the flesh. We must be aware that we are continually being bombarded by the enemy on all three fronts.

When I lived in Germany, I daily faced the battle on all three fronts during an ordinary circumstance of life. Every day I would jog four miles in the neighborhood. Around the corner from my home was a theater. The Germans are much more public in their display of nudity and pornography than I was accustomed. Occasionally on the theater advertisement boards they would display pornographic pictures. When I jogged by the theater I was often confronted with a battle on each of the three levels.

First, there was spiritual warfare. Satan tempted and enticed. He would whisper into my ears his lies, "Why don't you look? No one will know. You won't hurt anyone else. It'll be your little secret." Next, there was the battle within myself. To be honest, my flesh wanted to look. My eyes wanted to lust. But I had a choice to make: obey the Spirit of God or obey the lusts of my flesh. Finally, I battled with a system around me that was anti-God. Such a system always demeans human life. To view such pornography would be buying into a world system that treats women like objects to be used for man's own pleasure. It was completely contrary to the teachings of the Bible, which treats women with dignity as a fellow heir of the grace of life. Therefore, I needed to learn to fight the enemy on all three fronts. I had to, first, humble myself under God's mighty hand and resist the devil. I had to acknowledge every day that I needed God. Without Him I could do nothing. As I submitted to Him, I had the power to resist the temptations of Satan. Then, I had to make a concrete decision to die to the desires of my flesh. As I jogged past that theater, I would point my eyes toward the ground and pray, "I choose against the flesh, and I choose Jesus." I would continue to pray in that manner until I was past the theater.

Finally, I would thank God for women who were "fellow heirs of the grace of life." I would allow my mind to be renewed by thinking on those things that were pleasing to God. I experienced victory over the subtle ways of Satan because I learned to do battle on all three fronts. Many believers find themselves defeated because they haven't learned to fight on all three fronts.

KNOW YOURSELF

Not only must we know God intimately and know the schemes of the devil, but we need to be well acquainted with our own selves. Everyone of us has weaknesses and strengths. Normally Satan launches an all-out attack at our point of weakness. Many believers face continual struggle in certain areas of their lives and never seem to have victory. Satan seems to launch a nonstop attack on that particular area of our lives. Just the moment that we think we have victory, we find ourselves defeated.

I have been personally encouraged and greatly helped by 1 Corinthians 10:12–13: "Therefore, let him who thinks he stands take heed lest he fall. . . . and God is faithful, who will not allow you to be tempted beyond what you are able." We need to take heed or acknowledge and be keenly aware of the weak areas of our lives. As we acknowledge and surrender them to God, we become wholly dependent upon Him. And we will find that God will prevail and be faithful to give us victory in every temptation.

However, when we begin to ignore those weak areas of our lives as though we can find victory in our own strength, we meet defeat. In many instances we may need to not only make ourselves accountable to God, but we may also need to become accountable to other Christians with our areas of weaknesses. Knowing our weaknesses places us in a position to draw on the strength of God and others.

> *[Satan] . . . is much more subtle in his attack on our strengths. He . . . tells us how good we are doing. He magnifies our strengths until they become weaknesses.*

But we also need to be aware of our strengths. Satan normally attacks us directly at our point of weakness, but he is much more subtle in his attack on our strengths. He simply pats us on the back and tells us how good we are doing. He magnifies our strengths until they become weaknesses. He accomplishes this in two different ways. First, he builds pride into our hearts. We cease depending upon God and begin depending on our own abilities. We compare ourselves to others who are not so strong in that area of their lives and pride arises in our hearts. That can be fatal. Humility is the first line of defense in the heart of the Christian. William Gurnall offers some solid advice. "Knowing your strength lies wholly in God and not in yourself, remain humble—even when God is blessing and using you most. Remember, when you have your best suit on, who made it and who paid for it!"[1]

I am convinced that in every example of the fallen soldiers previously mentioned, Satan first weaseled into their hearts through pride. Once pride filled their hearts, they were wide open for the onslaught of Satan. James says, "God is opposed to the proud, but gives grace to the humble." He makes that statement immediately before telling the believer to "resist the devil." If Satan can make us proud about our strengths, then he has effectively made us incapable of resisting him.

The second way in which Satan uses our strengths is to magnify them so that they spill into other areas of our lives where they become weaknesses. Everyone's strength can also be his or her weakness. For instance, God had to work deeply in my life to break me at my point of strength. He has gifted me with certain oratorical abilities and debating skills. He uses those abilities in the international ministry to which He has called me. As a result, many have come to Christ. However, those strengths have many times been my weak points in dealing with interpersonal relationships. I've had a tendency to use those God given abilities to prove my point and get my way in those relationships. I've had to learn to recognize that strength as a weakness and trust God for His victory.

The more we know and understand ourselves, the more capable we are of experiencing Christ's victory in those areas of our lives. We can be on guard and place spiritual protection around our hearts and lives. There are six areas of our lives over which every Christian should place a close guard. Be attentive to those six areas, for they are places where Satan normally attacks frequently. Knowing yourself means recognizing and monitoring your thoughts, feelings, speech, relationships, time, and energy. Let's look at those six.

Guard your thoughts. The greatest battle in the Christian life normally takes place in the mind. That's why Paul stated, "We are taking every thought captive to the obedience of Christ" (2 Corinthians 10:5b). Satan continually attacks with thoughts that are negative, vain, incorrect, and unholy. We must learn to take those thoughts captive to the obedience of Christ and His Word. But how does one practically do that? First, know the Word of God. Reject any thought that does not match up to His Word. Second, refuse vain speculations. Don't allow vain imaginations to capture your thinking. Third, choose to think on "whatever is true, whatever is honorable, whatever is right, whatever is pure, whatever is lovely, whatever is of good repute" (Philippians 4:8). Whatever you allow into your inner life through reading, listening, seeing, or feeling, make sure that it passes the test of pleasing God.

Guard your feelings. God created us with emotions. We don't need to be afraid of them. They can be the source of great positive experiences in our lives. However, they also can become very destructive. Satan knows the power of human emotions. Therefore, he will make every attempt to attack us through our emotions. Two primary ways in which you can protect your emotions is to forgive others and let the Holy Spirit control you. First, practice forgiveness. When you sin, don't procrastinate in confessing and repenting of your sins. The longer that you put it off, the more entangled your feelings become with guilt, fear, and insecurity. Those negative feelings give place to Satan to play havoc in your life. But, also, forgive others. A refusal to forgive others will damage your own emotions. Bitterness habored in the human heart can only produce suffering and hurt. Draw deeply from the well of God's grace regularly and forgive those who have wronged you.

More damage has been done to the Christian community by rumors spread by believers than by persecution spread by evil dictators.

The second way in which we can guard our emotions is by being filled with the Holy Spirit. The fruit of the Spirit, as described in Galatians 5:22–23, is mainly human emotion: "love, joy, peace, patience, kindness, goodness, faithfulness, gentleness, self control." As we yield ourselves to the control of the Holy Spirit, He fills us with the very life of Christ. We then experience those emotions that are both positive and powerful. The Holy Spirit not only guards our emotions but also transforms them. All of us have been wounded in our hearts at one time or another. Some of us have been wounded more deeply. But the Holy Spirit has the power to heal and restore our emotions to that which God created them to be.

Guard your speech. The tongue has more power to do damage to our lives than perhaps any other part of our body. James says, "And the tongue is a fire, the very world of iniquity; the tongue is set among our members as that which defiles the entire body, and sets on fire the course of our life, and is set on fire by hell" (James 3:6). Pretty strong words! We must recognize the power of our speech. We have the power to bless or destroy other lives by the use of our tongues.

Sometimes I think that many Christians think other Christians are the enemy. Often we spend more time fighting one another with our tongues than we do proclaiming the kingdom of God. The tongue has great power—to proclaim the great message of salvation to all men everywhere or to leave the church in absolute confusion and disarray. The serious soldier of Jesus Christ needs to set a guard over his tongue. I offer five suggestions: (1) be slow to speak and quick to listen; (2) don't repeat rumors. I'm convinced that more damage has been done to the Christian community by rumors spread by believers than by persecution spread by evil dictators; (3) be honest in your speech; (4) be positive in your speech; (5) and ask yourself, "Would Jesus be pleased with what I am saying?"

Guard your relationships. I have seen young people on fire for God with a deep commitment to live as soldiers of the cross. Then they enter into a relationship with someone who doesn't have the same commitment to Christ and, consequently, lose their fervor to reach the world for Christ.

Garland McKee was the pastor under whose ministry I came to Christ and surrendered my life to preach the gospel; he officiated at my wedding to Tex. I hadn't seen him in years when we reunited recently at a conference where I spoke. Afterward, we had coffee and were reminiscing about the many things that God had done in my life over the last twenty-five years. One frank comment caught my attention: "You realize that you would not have been able to accomplish any of those things if it had not been for Tex," McKee said. "Without her wholehearted support, it would have been impossible." He was absolutely right. My wife supported my relationship with God.

The wrong kind of relationship, however, will spell disaster for the soldier of Christ. But God-ordained and Christ-centered relationships can be used mightily of God. This holds not only true in the marriage relationship but also in working relationships in the spreading of the kingdom of God. One reason God has used evangelist Billy Graham so effectively is because of the team that was knit together early in his ministry. They were men and women of common vision, concern, and passion. Because they were bound together in a Christ-centered relationship, they have impacted the world for Christ.

Guard your time. Satan has subtly disarmed the church of Jesus Christ by rocking her to sleep in the bed of wasted time. Time is the most precious of human commodities. Technology can be reproduced, buildings rebuilt, and organization restructured. But once time escapes us, it is gone forever.

Too many Christians in the West have become couch potatoes rather than soldiers of the most high God. I'm afraid a survey of American Christians comparing their time spent viewing television with the time spent studying the Word of God would prove extremely embarrassing. Paul said, "mak[e] the most of your time, because the days are evil" (Ephesians 5:16). These are historic days in which we are living. Once they have passed, we will never again have the same opportunity to further the kingdom of God as we do today. We must be very careful to place a guard over our time. The enemy would like nothing more than to steal it from us.

Guard your energy. I have discovered that I am most susceptible to defeat in my Christian life when I become exhausted. There's the tendency to become irritable when I'm tired. It becomes easy to respond in the flesh and give place to the enemy. There's nothing wrong with hard work and becoming tired from a heavy schedule. However, when our schedules are so full that we consistently don't have time to think, pray, and rest, then we open ourselves to the attacks of the enemy. Military forces have learned to exhaust prisoners when they want to brainwash them. The cults quite often methodically deprive people of sleep when they want to convince people of their false teachings. We must understand that we're more susceptible to demonic deception when we're exhausted.

I've had to learn to set aside time for rest when I come home from an exhausting trip. If I don't take time to renew myself physically and spiritually, then I find myself struggling in my interpersonal relationships and my fellowship with God. God created us with a need for renewal. If we don't live in accordance with His plans, we will find ourselves in deep trouble.

Finally, in preserving your energy and guarding yourself from spiritual attack, recognize that Satan most often attacks in the small details of our lives and plans of ministry. Many times I have seen great plans to reach out to those in darkness fall apart because of a lack of attention to details. Satan will find one weak area and exploit it for all that its worth. The smallest area of neglect often becomes the greatest attack of the enemy. Perhaps that's why Jesus taught His disciples to learn to be faithful in the smallest of things in their lives.

The Christian who gets to know his God, his enemy, and himself will have found a shelter, a fortress, and a shield. He will discover that God Himself will be his defender. The safest place in the world is in the center of God's will. Arise, soldier, and put on the whole armor of God! You don't have to fear what the enemy can do. Your God will lead you. He will be your fortress in the heat of the battle.

There is not a temptation which the Word of God does not arm you against.

William Gurnall
The Christian in Complete Armour

For the weapons of our warfare are not of the flesh, but divinely powerful for the destruction of fortresses.

2 Corinthians 10:4

8

The Weapons
of the Soldier

I walked alone on the South African beach late one evening. My heart was heavy. Each evening I had spoken in the Durban church, and God seemed to be working deeply in hearts of listeners. But there were so many who hadn't yet received the gospel. When I first drove into Durban, I had seen the large sign on one of the buildings saying, "Welcome to Islam."

Now as I walked the shoreline and prayed I asked God, "How can we reach the Muslim community? There are so many that need Your love."

I left the cooling breezes of that African shore to head back to the hotel. On my way, I walked along the sand and noticed a crowd of people. Some sort of debate seemed to be taking place, and I stopped to listen. A group of Christians were attempting to present the gospel to three Muslim men. I couldn't believe what I heard. The Muslims appeared to know more about the Bible than the Christians. They kept saying, "We believe only the words of Jesus. We don't believe what Paul said about Jesus. He distorted the teachings of Jesus. Therefore, we can only accept what Jesus said. And Jesus never said that he would die on a cross in Jerusalem. That is a myth that grew up from the followers of Jesus."

I kept waiting for the Christians to give a response. But none came. The Muslims had the Christians backed in the corner with nowhere to turn. Finally, I spoke up.

"Excuse me. I know that I'm not a part of this conversation. But could I say something that I think would be helpful?"

"Certainly," everyone responded.

I then asked the Muslims, "Do you really believe the words of Jesus—all of them?"

"Yes, of course we do."

"Then please permit me to show you a passage of Scripture," I begged. I then turned to Matthew 20:18–19 and began to read the words of Jesus. "Behold, we are going up to Jerusalem; and the Son of Man will be delivered to the chief priests and scribes, and they will condemn Him to death, and will deliver Him to the Gentiles to mock and scourge and crucify Him, and on the third day He will be raised up." I also pointed them to Matthew 16:21, which says, "From that time Jesus Christ began to show His disciples that He must go to Jerusalem, and suffer many things from the elders and chief priests and scribes, and be killed, and be raised up on the third day."

The Muslims were almost speechless. "We've never seen that in the Bible," they stuttered. Then they began to attack Christianity from another perspective. "Do you believe that Jesus is equal to the Father?" they asked. "If you do, then you believe in two Gods—not one. Coequality connotes plurality. Therefore, you Christians believe in three Gods."

"Let me ask you a question," I responded. "Is there a spiritual part of your life?"

"Yes, of course," they enthusiastically answered.

I continued to probe. "Is there a part of your life that could be defined as personality—with mind, emotions, and will—that is distinctive from the spiritual part of your life?"

"Yes."

"And is there a physical part of your life that is distinct from your personality and spirituality?" I asked.

"Yes, there is."

Then I looked one of them straight in the eyes and said, "There must be three of you—not one."

They laughed and said, "OK, OK, we get your point." We discussed faith in Christ for another hour. When we started to leave they shook my hand and said, "We have never met anyone before who could answer our questions about the Bible. You have given us much to think about."

I make no claims to be a Bible scholar. But I believe every Christian can be an effective and serious student of the Bible. Otherwise, we are like soldiers who go out to battle without any weapons. Those South African Christians on the beach that night had the right idea. They wanted to be in the battle for the souls of mankind. However, when they arrived at the battlefield, they found themselves totally unprepared to rightly handle the weapon that had been entrusted them.

They aren't unusual. We live in a generation in the West that has grossly neglected the grand old truths of the Bible. In the modern evangelical church, doctrine is out and experience is in. I'm afraid that we've raised an entire generation of believers who are biblically illiterate. While we have been attempting to battle secularism, numerous cults have risen. Islam has become the fastest growing religion in the world. And the church struggles to respond.

From my personal experiences in Eastern Europe, I don't feel that secularism is the greatest weapon of the enemy against the church. False religion is a much more formidable piece of artillery in Satan's arsenal. Secularism leaves a vacuum in the hearts of people. But false religion attempts to fill that vacuum with the errors and lies of hell.

God has given the church weapons that are divinely powerful and quite capable of silencing every weapon formed against the church. Four powerful weapons are at the Christian's disposal: the Bible, the message of the cross, the testimony of believers, and a surrendered life. These four weapons are able to destroy every thing that lifts itself up against the true knowledge of God. When the Christian begins to familiarize himself with these weapons, the gates of hell begin to tremble. Satan knows that he is no match for the mighty weapons of God.

THE BIBLE

When Paul listed the Christian's defensive armor in Ephesians 6, he only listed one offensive weapon—"the sword of the Spirit, which is the word of God" (verse 17b). The Bible is the sword that performs surgery on the heart of the Christian, exposing his sin and carefully purging it from his life. This sword shows the believer when He's gotten off the highway of holiness and then points him back to the straight and narrow path. As God's light in a dark world, it teaches him how to stay on the path of righteousness.

Before freedom came to Eastern Europe, Satan tried to keep the Bible out of that part of the world. However, since the new freedoms, he has changed his strategy. If he can't keep the Bible from the people, he will attempt to distort, pervert, and change it. Members of the Church of Jesus Christ of the Latter-Day Saints (Mormons) have flooded into Eastern Europe. They arrive saying, "We also believe the Bible. But we have another book. Because it was given to man later than the Bible, it's the final authority." Jehovah's Witnesses have been just as aggressive in saying that they believe the Bible also. "But," they say, "we have a better translation."

If we are to win the battle for this generation, we must once again become a people of the Bible. We must read, study, and obey the Bible.

As I preach in the far regions of Russia, the most frequently asked questions by new believers are ones about astrology, Jehovah's Witnesses, and Mormons. Satan has aggressively planted his seeds to the most remote regions of Eastern Europe. For instance, when I first visited Mongolia there were only seventy-five Christians in the nation, and I had an unusual conversation with a man on the street. I had been teaching a conference on prayer to the new believers. Only the New Testament had been translated into the Mongolian language at that time, and Christianity had been presented to the people only recently.

As I walked down the street, a man came running up to me and he spoke in simple English. "Excuse me, sir. Are you from America?"

"Yes," I responded.

"Oh," he said. "I have been to America."

I thought that was quite unusual. "Where did you visit?" I asked.

"Salt Lake City, Utah. You see," he said, "I'm translating the Book of Mormon into the Mongolian language."

I couldn't believe it! The whole Bible wasn't even translated yet, and the cults were busy attempting to steal the hearts of a people who were without the gospel. I've told the people of Eastern Europe that the great issue before freedom came was the Bible. And the great issue since these new days of democracy is still the Bible. Satan continues to do everything he can to keep this powerful weapon out of the hands and hearts of God's people.

To a great extent believers in the West are biblically illiterate. If we are to win the battle for this generation, we must once again become a people of the Bible. We must read, study, and obey the Bible. The homes of most Western Christians have the Bible in them, but the heart of the average Western Christian remains empty and void of the Word of God; he cannot use it properly for spiritual battle.

Every great revival in history has returned people to the Scriptures. They were preached, studied, and obeyed. Society was impacted. The light of God's Word dispelled the darkness.

Christians commonly look to one of four sources of authority within the church. Some use *tradition* as their source of authority. Tradition is simply what is passed down from one generation to the next. It's believing and acting one way because our forefathers did it that way. The second source of authority for many believers is *experience.* Many evangelical Christians have begun to live as though experience is their final source of authority. The third source for many people is *a person.* Not only do many Catholic Christians rely on such a source, but I have met many evangelicals who have adopted a system of little popes. Their source of authority becomes whatever their leader tells them. All three sources of authority are inadequate for the true believer in Jesus Christ. The final source of authority for life and faith for the Christian must be *the Bible.*

All experience must align itself with the Scripture, or we may find ourselves deceived. The only tradition that has eternal value is that tradition rooted in the Word of God. And the test of any "spokesman for God" must be that what he says is in agreement with the Scripture. The Bible is the only valid, final source of authority for the follower of Jesus Christ. If we are to be victorious soldiers on the battlefield of life, then we must be men and women of that one great book, the Bible.

Gurnall said to the ministers in his generation, "A thousand quips and quotable clichés will not end Satan's control over lives. But draw the sword of the Word and strike with its naked edge—this is the only way to pierce your people's consciences and spill the blood of their sins."[1] We would do well to take his advice today. That great sword has been used throughout the ages to defeat the enemy and capture nations for Christ. It remains as effective today as it has throughout the centuries.

The apostle John mentions the other three weapons that have been given to the soldier of Jesus Christ in Revelation 12. Here John describes a great battle between Satan and the saints of God. He then tells how the believers overcame Satan.

THE MESSAGE OF THE CROSS

The first weapon John cites is "the blood of the Lamb." Satan trembles at the message of the cross. In it lies the very power of God to forgive men's sins, set captive hearts free, and bring eternal life to those separated from God. Normally Satan attempts to distort or deny certain biblical teachings: the deity of Christ, the Bible as the Word of God, and the cross as God's provision for man's salvation. That's why the Muslims on that South African beach wanted to deny that Jesus actually died on the cross. If there is no death, then there can be no forgiveness of sins. But Christ took the punishment for our sins by dying on the cross. To an unbelieving mind, that may sound really foolish. But to those of us who know Christ, the message of the cross of Christ becomes the very power of God.

I remain amazed at the power of the simple message of the cross of Christ. In 1989 I was leading a prayer seminar at the Lausanne Congress on World Evangelization in Manila, the Philippines. At the close of the seminar, many people had gathered around me to talk. At the back of the group stood a lady waiting patiently to speak with me. Finally, when everyone was gone, she asked me, "Are you the same Sammy Tippit that was arrested in Chicago in 1971 for witnessing of Christ in the Rush Street district?"

I was surprised by her question. "Yes, that's me," I said. But I wondered who she was and how she knew about that incident. I remembered that ministry in Chicago during the early seventies, working with runaway youth, street gangs, and drug addicts. On occasions, my friends and I went to the night club district of Chicago to pass out gospel tracts and present our faith in Christ. Many people accepted Christ into their hearts, and the message of Christ began to penetrate that dark area of Chicago. Consequently, the clubs that normally closed at 4:00 A.M. began to close at midnight because of a lack of business. The frustrated owners of one particular club wanted us off the street, so they had some policemen arrest us. We eventually went to trial, and the city of Chicago admitted to false arrest and dropped the charges. But how would a participant in this congress so far from Chicago know all of that?

"Tell me, how do you know about my time in Chicago?"

"Well," she said, "I was a go-go dancer in one of those night clubs. One night you gave me a gospel tract. I took it and read it. I actually came out to hear you speak one evening, and I eventually gave my heart to Christ. I left the clubs and now I am married. My husband and I are missionaries. I've prayed for years that God would one day let me meet you again to say 'thank you' for bringing the message of God's salvation to me. God answered my prayer today. So, thank you for bringing the message of the cross to the night clubs of Chicago."

I was dumbfounded. . . . A simple message of Christ dying for the sins of the world took a woman out of the dark dens of iniquity and made her a flaming evangel.

The lady then turned and walked away. I was left dumbfounded. I wept and thanked God for her encouraging words. But I stood in awe at the power of the message of the cross. A simple message of Christ dying for the sins of the world took a woman out of the dark dens of iniquity and made her a flaming evangel of the good news of Christ's love.

I have seen the hardest drug addicts transformed by the cross's powerful message. I have watched gang members changed by faith in the cross. I've seen racial hatred turn into racial harmony by the power of the cross. Guilt and bitterness have fallen from distressed hearts as the message of the cross penetrated deeply into the souls of men and women. Oh, what a weapon that has been given to God's people: "They overcame him by the blood of the Lamb" (Revelation 12:11a).

THE TESTIMONY OF BELIEVERS

Next, the apostle says we overcome Satan by "the word of our testimony" (Revelation 12:11b). This means we proclaim that powerful message of the cross. When one trusts in the finished work of Christ on the cross, his life will never be the same. His eternal destiny will never be the same. God can mightily use the testimony of what Christ has done in our lives. Every believer has a testimony to share.

If our sins have been forgiven, then we have great things about which to speak. The Christian who learns to utilize this weapon will experience victory over the enemy and joy in his heart.

Early in my ministry, Tex presented the good news of Christ to a girl who was a drug addict. Connie was facing thirty years in prison for sale and use of marijuana and other illegal drugs. This girl had been in and out of drug rehabilitation centers and had visited psychologists, but nothing seemed to work. Now she was deeply involved in witchcraft. Tex told Connie of God's love for her, and Connie could hardly believe it. Later, she came to hear me speak. She wanted to talk with me after the service.

"I'm in bondage," she said bluntly. "My lover is drugs. I live for them. I've tried everything to get off. But there's no hope for me. Can Jesus help me?"

Tex and I told her of the power of the cross. That night she placed her faith in Jesus and what He did on the cross. Connie didn't have any great mystical experience. She simply took God at His word. And God worked a miracle in her life that night. She went home and flushed all of her drugs down the toilet. Christ set her free! The judge was so impressed with the change in her life that he released her to Tex's and my custody. From that day until now, Connie has been liberated from the power of drugs.

She was so excited about what God had done in her life that she said to me, "Being forgiven and set free is so wonderful that I just wish I could have that same experience every day!"

I laughed and said, "Connie, what God has done for you is permanent. But there's one thing that is almost as wonderful as coming to Christ."

"What's that?" she eagerly asked.

"It's telling someone what Christ has done for you," I told her. "When someone else comes to Christ because you shared your testimony with them, it will be some of the deepest joy that you will have in life."

It wasn't long until Connie came running up to me saying, "Sammy, you're right! You're right! I've just told someone what Christ has done for me and they too wanted Christ. I've never known such deep joy!"

I've seen God again and again use the verbalizing of a personal testimony to invade the enemy's territory and liberate souls from the chains of darkness. It's such a simple weapon, but a powerful one. It's a weapon with which every Christian has been equipped.

The power of the spoken testimony
is not in how bad we've been.
The dynamic of the testimony is
in how good and great God is.

Some may disagree, saying, "I wasn't a drug addict. I don't have a dynamic testimony. I grew up in a Christian home and never did anything really bad. I don't think my testimony would make much of a difference in people's lives."

That's a lie straight out of hell. Satan would love to have you believe that. If he convinces you that your testimony is ineffective, then he's kept you from using a weapon that can do great damage to the kingdom of darkness. It took the same blood of Jesus to forgive your sins as it did to forgive the drug addict or gang leader. The power of the spoken testimony is not in how bad we've been. The dynamic of the testimony is in how good and great God is.

Here are some general suggestions about testifying for Christ as well as a practical outline of how to give your testimony. First, *be honest*. Don't try to make yourself out to be someone that isn't really you. God's Spirit will only use that which is truthful, and people respond to you when they sense genuineness. Second, *be brief*. State clearly and concisely what has happened to you. Third, *use terms that are understandable* to the non-Christian. Remember, most non-Christians are completely unfamiliar with the Christian's vocabulary. Speak with simplicity and humility of heart. People won't listen to one who speaks with a spirit of arrogance.

The following is a simple outline for presenting your testimony that I've seen God use in many different situations in many cultures. It may be helpful to you.

I. Tell a little about your life before you came to Christ.
II. Mention some of the events that led you to Christ.
III. Present your actual salvation experience. Be especially clear at this point. Avoid statements that are not understandable to non-Christians such as, "I walked down the aisle during the invitation." The average non-Christian won't have the slightest idea what you are talking about.
IV. Speak of the change that Christ has made in your life. Don't overstate or understate it. If you came to know Christ at a young age, and there was no dramatic change, then say that honestly. Tell how Christ has given you strength throughout your life. People will respect and listen to a genuine and honest testimony.

A SURRENDERED LIFE

The final weapon listed by the apostle John is the life surrendered to Christ: "They did not love their lives, even unto death" (Revelation 12:11c). Our testimony is made understandable by the way in which we live. People understand devotion and commitment. A friend recently told me about a person who said one thing but lived another. "I quit listening to what this person said, and I began listening to his actions. Their actions told me clearly the truth about that person."

Many people in Western society are confused about Christianity because they have watched many Christians proclaim one way of life and live altogether another way. It's only when our walk matches our talk that the gospel becomes clear to a dark and desperate world. Herein lies a great difference in the church in Eastern Europe and the church in the West. Western Christians are tuned into the information age. We have adapted a philosophy that says, "The more information that one has, the more power he has." Consequently, we fill our notebooks, attend conferences, and seek to have the latest "insight" to some new truth. But somehow we've forgotten that truth must be obeyed, or we have accomplished nothing except to deceive ourselves.

On the other hand, Christians in Eastern Europe who fought and won the battle were men and women with limited access to information. The mighty weapon with which they fought so valiantly was the life surrendered to God. The message of Christ is believable and easily understood to the present generation of Eastern European Christians because of how that message was lived by the previous generation. They had no political clout, but they had tremendous spiritual power. They lived what they believed, no matter the cost. If it meant losing their jobs, going to jail, or dying for their faith, they were ready to pay the price. Many of them never lived to see this historic moment. But they made the gospel understandable to this generation by their surrendered lives.

God has given us weapons that are capable of destroying the strongest fortresses of Satan. When we begin to utilize them, we will see light dispel the darkness and victory in the midst of the battle. Take up your weapons, soldiers of Christ. Invade the enemy's territory and claim this generation for Christ.

Prayer, and more prayer, adds to the fighting quali-
ties and the more certain victories of God's good
fighting men. The power of prayer is most forceful on
the battlefield amid the din and strife of conflict.

E. M. Bounds
The Necessity of Prayer

With all prayer and petition pray at all times in the
Spirit, and with this in view, be on the alert with all
perseverance and petition for all the saints.

Ephesians 6:18

9

The Weapon
of Prayer

Not many people were on the American Airlines flight to
Frankfurt, Germany. As a matter of fact, I almost had the entire
plane to myself. President George Bush had "drawn a line in the
sand" and warned Saddam Hussein to remove his troops from
Kuwait or face the consequences of military actions. Hussein
dug in and refused to heed Bush's challenge. Within a day of
my arrival in Germany, the war commenced. Many people were
fearful of international travel and terrorist attacks, and the plane
had lots of empty seats.

My arrival in Germany was uneventful, and I proceeded to
an American military base where I would minister. At times I
listened to broadcasts over the military radio and television
about the war's progress. The allied forces had unleashed a tor-
rent of air bombardment against the Iraqis. The commanders
then began to speak of a ground attack that would be launched.
The terminology used was intriguing. Allied commanders said
that the ground battle would not commence until the air attack
had moved to another level. They said, "We definitely have *air
superiority*, but the ground attack won't begin until we have
achieved *air supremacy*. Air supremacy will ensure that we will
have the fewest possible casualties when the ground forces begin their assault."

In effect, the allied commanders were saying that there was absolutely no question who had the strongest and most capable air power. The allies were far more powerful than the Iraqis. However, they knew that the enemy could inflict great damage to the ground troops unless the Iraqis were rendered absolutely powerless to attack the allies from the air. As I thought about the statements of the allied commanders, I thought to myself, *Christians could learn from the allied commanders a great lesson in spiritual warfare.*

A battle rages in the heavenly places for the hearts and souls of mankind. There is no doubt that the church has air superiority. Christ in us is far greater than Satan who enslaves the hearts of men and women. The air attack that the Christian launches is that of intercessory prayer. The ground attack comes from those foot soldiers entering the enemy's territory to share their faith in Jesus Christ. However, before any ground attack is launched we would do well to tarry in prayer until we have the absolute assurance that the battle in the heavenly places has been won. We already have *air superiority*. But we must know that we have achieved *air supremacy* before the assault is launched to free the captives of Satan's army. Satan must be rendered helpless before the evangelistic thrust is launched.

I'm convinced that many of those recently fallen Christian leaders met defeat because they didn't understand this principle of warfare. They attempted to assault the kingdom of darkness without having first won the battle in the heavenly places through prayer. They became overdependent upon technology and talent and underdependent upon God. They forgot that the battle is basically a spiritual one and must first be won in the realm of the spirit. Much tragedy and disgrace could have been avoided if they would have understood in the spiritual realm what the allied commanders understood in the physical.

My ministry of evangelism consists to a great extent of penetrating virgin enemy territory. Often I am in cities and nations where there has never been a proclamation of the gospel in an open public setting. I'm convinced that we must first achieve air supremacy through prayer before we attempt to bring the message of Christ to those who have never heard the good news. The battle will be won because God has gone ahead of us preparing the way. He has not called me or any of us to be super salesmen, but rather soldiers of the cross.

The first time I preached the gospel openly in a stadium in the former Soviet Union was a thrilling experience. I had been arrested several years earlier because I had told university students about Christ. I was very anxious about what kind of reception I would have in an open stadium. It was September 1990 in Belt'cy, Moldavia, a city of about 150,000. At first the city council refused the Christians permission to conduct the evangelistic meetings. The believers appealed to the Supreme Council of Soviet Moldavia, and the Supreme Council overruled the city council and gave us permission for one afternoon in the stadium.

I didn't know what to anticipate. Would the people come to the stadium? Would they respond to the message? When I met with the Belt'cy pastors at the church immediately prior to going to the stadium, I asked them what they were anticipating. *Perhaps*, I thought, *they're wondering whether the platform be in the center of the stadium, facing one side. Or that it be at one end, facing both sides. Are they expecting the entire stadium to be filled, or are they hoping for half of the stadium?*

None of the above. Instead, the pastors replied, "We believe that God is going to fill the stadium with atheists. Therefore, we have told the Christians not to sit in the stadium. They must leave room for the non-Christians." I must admit that I didn't have that kind of faith. But I took them at their word. When we arrived at the stadium, I couldn't believe my eyes. The stadium was packed, and another 3,000 people were standing.

I stood on the platform that afternoon and began to preach. In the middle of my message, a bottle of water exploded (for no apparent reason) on the platform. A few minutes later, all the electrical power went out. No one could hear me. For fifteen minutes I stood in silence while men scurried; finally, they found and repaired the problem. I began to preach again, but with a keen realization that we were in the midst of a raging battle—a spiritual battle—for the hearts and minds of the men and women of this city.

At the close of my message, I invited people to turn from sin and place their faith in Jesus Christ. "If you are willing to repent of your sins and place your faith in Christ, would you please lift your hands?" I asked. "I will pray that God will work deeply in your hearts." I scanned the stadium, but no one lifted a hand.

I prayed, "Oh, God, what should I do now?" I decided to continue the appeal for people to place their faith in Jesus. "I would like to pray with you today," I said. "If you are willing to believe in Jesus and invite Him into your life, I'm going to ask you to come to the front of the platform and allow me to lead you in a prayer of repentance and faith."

The real heroes of heaven are not going to be the "platform people." They will be the people who. . . pray with the passion of Christ for a lost world.

No one came; I felt heartbroken. I didn't know what to do. I bowed my head in prayer. When I looked up, I saw a poor peasant woman leaving the stands and marching all by herself to the platform. She was carrying a bouquet of flowers high over her head. She looked almost like the lady holding aloft the torch in America's fabled Statue of Liberty. The woman marched all alone to the front of the platform and handed me the flowers. Then she immediately fell to her knees and began to cry unto God.

The moment that she hit her knees, people began to leave the stands and come to the platform—in tens, fifties, and even in groups of hundreds. They continued to come until about 2,500 people, weeping and expressing their desire to place their faith in Jesus, stood before me. It was a beautiful and humbling experience.

An Answered Prayer

When I returned to the United States, we described the poor peasant woman in our ministry newsletter. One lady who receives our newsletter is also a part of a women's prayer group which had been praying for our Moldavian crusade for several months. Caron called my office and asked, "Sammy, can I come by your office? I've just read your newsletter, and there's something that I must show you."

When she arrived, she pulled out her prayer journal. Daily she had recorded those things for which she had been praying and how God had impressed her to pray. For two months prior to the crusade in Moldavia, Caron had written in her journal, "Oh God, I pray for a peasant woman in Moldavia that she would have the courage to do whatever you are telling her to do." When I read in her journal that God consistently impressed her to pray for a peasant woman to be courageous, I was overwhelmed. It convinced me that the real heroes of heaven are not going to be the "platform people." They won't necessarily be the D. L. Moodys, the Charles Finneys, or the Billy Grahams. The real heroes of heaven will be those unknown to man, but well known to God. They will be the people who have that intimate relationship with Him, who pray with the passion of Christ for a lost world.

We must have a deep conviction that we have to be a people of prayer if we are to ever pierce the darkness around us. Sometimes I get the feeling that the evangelical Christian community in the West knows that prayer is a part of the Christian life. Therefore, we encourage people to pray. But I feel that we haven't seen the absolute necessity of prayer. It's not just the religious thing to do when we have an evangelistic outreach. Prayer is much more than that. It's foundational to piercing the darkness and reaching the world.

The Prayer Priority

When Jesus instituted the church, He told His followers to "wait in Jerusalem" prior to evangelizing the world. The disciples waited and prayed—the church was born from the position of prayer. Its health and strength were maintained through prayer. Study the book of Acts and you will discover that the secret to the growth and expansion of the church was found in its prayer meetings. In the early chapters of Acts, we continually find the church positioned in prayer. When Paul was thrust into Europe to reach the non-Jewish world, that call came in a prayer meeting (Acts 13). Why do we in the West then think that prayer is simply a sidelight to what we do? The real work of evangelism is prayer. It must not take a backseat in our work, but prayer must be maintained as a priority in the life of the church. Let me offer a few suggestions of how to make prayer a priority in your life and ministry.

Develop a Consistent Time Alone with God

Prayer is simply intimacy with God. God desires to have fellowship with His children. Above all else we need to have fellowship with our Father. The greatest culprit in robbing the church in the West of her intimacy with God is not allocating time for prayer. We're accustomed to rushing to a meeting, rushing through a meeting, and rushing out of a meeting to our next meeting that we have learned to do the same thing with God. One cannot be intimate with God and attempt to rush in and out of His presence.

During twenty-five years of marriage, my wife and I have attempted to develop and maintain our intimacy with each other. We've had to set aside time to be together, just the two of us. She's needed time to share the joys and hurts of her heart with me. And I've needed the same kind of time to reveal to her my deepest needs and greatest joys. When the Tippits don't take time for that, I've discovered that our relationship has a tendency to become strained. But when we make time for the intimate disclosure of our feelings and thoughts, then our relationship grows and is strengthened.

As believers we must understand that the same is true with our relationship to God. That relationship grows stronger as we make time to reveal the intimate needs of our hearts with Him and He reveals Himself to us. And a good, healthy, growing relationship with God is absolutely imperative if we are serious about piercing the darkness. Therefore, we must rearrange our priorities and our plans. If we're too busy for God, then we're just too busy.

Find a Prayer Partner

When I first became a Christian, I met weekly with three friends. We met at 6 A.M. to memorize Scripture together, tell each other our needs, and then pray. Those meetings accomplished several things in our lives. First, they encouraged each of us; they helped to stimulate us in our walk with God. Second, those meetings kept us accountable to each other in our personal growth. Third, they gave us courage to declare our faith in Christ with others; we began to reach our friends with the gospel. A citywide Christian youth movement resulted from those times of praying together. Finally, as a result of praying together we were able to pierce the darkness that surrounded us. A number of young people whose lives were filled with darkness came to know Christ. The light of the gospel went forth because of those days of prayer as a young Christian. I look back upon those days with the fondest of memories because God's presence was so real.

Attend the Prayer Meeting

Western Christians to a great extent have lost their vision for the old-time prayer meeting. God has used the prayer meeting throughout the history of the church to stir revival in the hearts of His people. When God's people begin to corporately seek His face, He begins to open the windows of heaven. Only a divine intervention in the affairs of Western civilization can dispel the darkness that is so prevalent in this decadent society. We have great examples in North America and Western Europe of God's intervention.

One of the greatest examples of God moving because of the prayer meeting was the great "prayer revival" of the mid-1800s. In the United States a series of prayer meetings began in Manhattan, New York, after businessman Jeremiah Lamphier called for a prayer meeting. At first only six people came. But God moved, and within six months more than 10,000 people were attending prayer meetings throughout New York City. The prayer meetings spread throughout North America until thousands of people in the United States and Canada were calling out to God for revival in the land. God sent His light in a great awakening; ministries began to flourish and the kingdom of God began to spread. Men such as D. L. Moody, Hudson Taylor, and Charles Spurgeon were all affected by the move of God's Spirit.

Believers in Northern Ireland still refer to [the 1859 prayer revival] as the year of grace. . . . In many areas of Ulster crime became virtually nonexistent.

About the same time God began to stir the hearts of the people of Britain to gather for prayer. In October 1857 four young men in Northern Ireland began a prayer meeting in a small schoolhouse outside a tiny village called Kells. That obscure schoolhouse became the birthplace of one of the greatest revivals in Ireland. After two years of prayer meetings a spiritual light burst forth, shattering the darkness. Almost 100,000 people received Christ as Savior during 1859. All of Britain was stirred for God. The believers in Northern Ireland still refer to it as the year of grace.

The revival affected every aspect of society, from social to moral to spiritual. In many areas of Ulster crime became virtually nonexistent as God's Spirit moved among the people. At the Quarter Sessions in Belfast in 1860 the assistant barrister, reporting in the local journals, wrote, "I have been enabled, in the first two towns of the county in which I held the Sessions, to congratulate the grand jury upon having nothing at all to do." The assistant barrister in Londonderry in April 1860 reported there was no criminal business. He was presented with white gloves.[1]

When I travel to Northern Ireland, I always stop in Kells and take a little time to meditate on the great things that God has done there. I'm always amazed at the smallness of Kells and that tiny schoolhouse. It doesn't take big numbers and great facilities for revival to begin. God normally looks for a small band of men and women who will join together to seek His face. Over one hundred years ago God's light filled four men in a small room outside a remote village in Northern Ireland. Darkness was pierced and the glory of God filled the land. Where are the men and women today who are willing to put aside some of their busyness and join together to seek the face of God? He is just as capable today as He was one hundred years ago of sending revival to His people.

Join the Prayer Movement

Something special is happening around the world today. God is moving. The church worldwide is experiencing more growth than she has ever known. The phenomenal growth in the church is being fostered by an unprecedented prayer movement. In Scotland 2,000 women pray weekly for revival through the national Prayer Chain ministry. In Korea tens of thousands of Christians awake at 4:00 each morning to be at 5 A.M. prayer meetings. Numerous U. S. cities are conducting regular Concerts of Prayer. In Brazil I have participated with more than 4,000 Baptist pastors and leaders who have begun prayer movements.

I continue to be amazed every month at the doors that God seems to be opening. During June 1993 I returned to Mongolia to speak and found a growing church. For 2,000 years Christianity has been forbidden or rejected there. Yet, in the past couple years the light of the gospel has burst forth upon that nation. The New Testament has been translated into Mongolian, and the Old Testament translation is now underway.

When I first visited Mongolia in 1991, I knew of only seventy-five believers meeting together. I had been asked by John Gibbens of Britain to hold a conference on prayer with these new believers. I met with forty of them at the airport my first day in the country.

"Who is the oldest Christian here?" I asked. A young man raised his hand. "How long have you been a Christian?"

"Four months," he replied.

I continued to probe. "Who is the newest Christian here?"

The young man next to me lifted his hand and said, "I've been a Christian for one day."

To teach biblical principles of prayer to those new believers was thrilling. They prayed with a sweetness and simplicity of heart for their nation. Less than two years later, more than 1,000 believers meet together. During my most recent visit I stood in the stadium in the capital city and preached outdoors for the first time in Mongolia.

How did all of this come about? We must credit a global prayer movement among Christians, a movement unprecedented in its scope and depth. It is strongest in developing nations; however, Christians in the West are beginning to catch the vision. For instance, "Meet You at the Pole" has become a major prayer event among students in U. S. high schools. For the past three years students have met before school one day in September to pray for revival in their school. It started in one region of the U. S. and has quickly become a national movement. An estimated 1.5 million students gathered around school flagpoles in September 1992 to pray for revival in their schools.[2] The national student and youth leaders say a new intensity exists among high school students, a strong desire to see a mighty revival sweep campuses.

I believe that young people and women have begun to catch the vision of what God can do when His people pray. However, I sense that men in the West as a whole have not yet seen what God can do through a prayer movement. Men in the West seem to feel that one must have measured results before he has really accomplished something of great value. However, we must realize that many of those men in Eastern Europe that God used never saw the positive outcomes for which they prayed.

But today their grandchildren are basking in the victory—a victory that was won by those prayers a generation earlier.

North America and the United Kingdom are big ships indeed. They won't be turned around overnight. Therefore, we should not look for instant results. Faith does not need that anyway. We must pray until revival comes or until Jesus comes.

THE POWER OF PRAYER

When a nation is engulfed in darkness, prayer can accomplish three things. First, it prepares the hearts of an unbelieving generation to receive the message of Christ. Multitudes were following Jesus because of the miracles He had performed. But then He told His listeners, "No one can come to me, unless the Father who sent Me draws him." If the miracles of Jesus couldn't change the state of the human heart, then I doubt that all the programs, talents, and strategies of evangelical Christians, by themselves, can make the transformation. The heart of man is in spiritual bondage and can be set free only by a deep work of the Holy Spirit.

That's why prayer is absolutely necessary to true conversion of the human heart. Prayer releases the Holy Spirit to convict people of their sins and draw them to Jesus.

When I first became a Christian I tried to present my faith in Christ to someone I loved. The person said he didn't want to hear about Christ. For more than twenty years I prayed for that person but honored his request that I not explain the gospel. One day two decades later, that person called and said, "I need God." Though he wouldn't let me explain the gospel for twenty years and wouldn't let me convince him of his need for God, the Holy Spirit was able to accomplish the impossible. Similarly, I have watched the hardened hearts of atheists melt under the convicting fire of the Holy Spirit when God's people pray. I've seen drug addicts, gang leaders, business persons, homemakers, and ordinary teenagers transformed because someone prayed. One day in heaven we will comprehend fully the vital role that prayer played in setting captive hearts free.

Second, Christians need to pray to have power to declare the news of the resurrected Christ. Fear is the biggest culprit robbing Christians of the joy of leading others to Christ. John says, however, that "perfect love casts out fear" (1 John 4:18). Thus we are made secure and confident in knowing His love; His love removes all fear. Because prayer is intimacy with God, we learn to bask in the love of God through those times of intimate communion; through such prayer we become courageous for Christ. The boldness of the church to declare Christ in a dark world will always be linked to intimacy with God. It will always be linked to prayer.

In my own relationship with God I have found the power to witness flowing from my intimacy with God. Sadly, I have found the opposite truth: When I don't take time for intimate communion with the Father, I become cowardly. Without sincere, intimate prayer, I've been intimidated, lacking the courage to proclaim Christ's love from the overflow of God's love.

Every great spiritual awakening in the history of the church has been preceded by a prayer movement.

The times in which we are living are unusual. The darkness seems overwhelming. The need of the hour is for soldiers who will courageously take the torch of the gospel into the center of the darkest parts of our world. Such courage comes from having been with God. There's no substitute for heart-to-heart communion with the Father.

Third, prayer releases the glory of God. Every great spiritual awakening in the history of the church has been preceded by a prayer movement. Prayer has a way of opening the windows of heaven and closing the gates of hell. The final result of prayer is the destruction of evil and the release of God's glory.

When Jesus taught the disciples to pray, the final thing He said was "do not lead us into temptation, but deliver us from evil. For Thine is the kingdom, and the power, and the glory, forever. Amen" (Matthew 6:13). He understood that prayer always leads to the glory of God. That's exactly the need of this generation—the glory of God among us. We don't need better methods or more beautiful buildings. Techniques can make our message more respectable, technology can broaden our influence, and buildings can give us room for the people. But only prayer will release the glory of God that dispels the darkness.

After twenty years of serving in the spiritually darkest parts of communist countries, I can summarize the one lesson I have learned: spiritual victory will only be achieved from the position of prayer. Prayer is more powerful than all the weapons that Satan can assemble against the church. Indeed, the gates of hell tremble when God's people pray. The darkness vanishes in an instant when God's glory is released.

One of the greatest testimonies to the power of prayer is the successful revolution in Romania. People who were maligned and considered the scum of the earth were able to bring down an evil dictatorial regime without lifting a hand against their enemies. They simply stood for the truth in love. They suffered—and they prayed. God released His glory and brought an entire nation to its knees. When will we learn in the West that it's the glory of God that we so desperately need?

If we're to capture our contemporaries for Christ, we must become a people of prayer. Prayer will prepare the hearts of an unbelieving generation to receive the gospel message. It will empower the believer to become a courageous witness for Christ. But most of all, prayer will release the glory of God. Let us cry unto God for His glory in these dark days.

Part 4

The Strategy for Battle

*Evangelist took him by the hand. "There is no sin,"
said he, "that God will not forgive, if you will believe
in Him."*

Christian stood up, trembling.

*"Listen carefully to what I say," said Evangelist.
"The man who deluded you was Mr. Worldly. His
name suits him because he is a man of the world
and goes to the town of Morality to church, for he
likes worldly wisdom better than the Cross. Therefore
this wicked man has turned you out of the right way.
The Lord says that you are to try to enter in at the
narrow gate—that is, the Wicket gate to which I have
sent you—for the narrow gate leads to life, and few
find it."*

John Bunyan
Pilgrim's Progress[1]

*Therefore if any man is in Christ, he is a new crea-
ture; the old things passed away; behold new things
have come.*

2 Corinthians 5:17

10

Changing
People's Hearts

We were exhausted. The four of us had been walking for twenty minutes, carrying heavy suitcases as we looked for the rental apartment where we would spend the night. Our long flight into Moscow had been uneventful, but we were now searching for the apartment in this Moscow suburb late at night—close to midnight, in fact. Our ultimate destination was Siberia. Eventually Titus, a Romanian, and Vasile, a Moldavian, would enter far eastern Siberia to arrange a forthcoming series of evangelistic meetings. Vladimir, a Russian, would accompany me to the Arctic Circle to preach in unreached cities. But during this layover we would rest and plan.

In the dark during a late hour in a foreign town, we were having trouble spotting the apartment. So one of us asked a lady for directions. To our relief, she said that we had finally arrived at the right apartment complex.

Then Titus asked her, "Ma'am, if you were to die tonight, do you know where you would spend eternity?"

I thought to myself, *Oh, come on, Titus. It's too late. We're infringing on this lady's kindness toward us.*

Then the lady responded, "No, I don't know. I'm from a Jewish family, but I have been taught atheism all of my life by our government."

Then I knew that I was right in my thinking. We were talking to a Jewish atheist. *It's no use talking to this lady,* I thought. *Let's go get some sleep. We have to get up at 5:00 in the morning, and I'm ready for bed!*

But even as I finished my thought, the lady continued, "Our government has failed us. I no longer believe what I've been taught. I want to know if there is a God and how I can know Him." For the next hour we discussed the Bible, her natural inclinations toward sin, and the hope of salvation through Jesus. At the close of our discussion she bowed her head and prayed with us. She asked Christ into her heart and placed her faith in Him. Did I ever feel guilty!

God had directed us to this lady. Now she directed us to the apartment that we were renting. An elderly lady was awaiting us. She was leasing the place to us for the evening and staying in her children's home. After she was paid and all the arrangements were settled, Vladimir asked her, "If you were to die tonight, do you have the assurance you will go to heaven?"

I thought, *Oh, come on, Vladimir. Not again. Not now! I'm tired. You're tired. She's tired. Let's be kind and give this poor lady some rest.*

But then the lady asked, "Can I really have eternal life? Tell me more." We had a conversation for thirty minutes; then there was a knock on the door.

I thought, *Who could it be at this time of night? I'll bet it's this little old lady's children coming to check on her. They're really going to be upset with us.* Wrong! It was the Jewish lady who had just prayed to receive Christ. She was so excited and filled with joy that she wanted to do something for us. She brought us food for breakfast, which was getting closer by the moment. And she wanted to hear more. So Titus was telling her more about her new faith, and Vladimir and Vasile were telling the elderly landlady about Christ. Finally the night of witnessing ended, and we were able to get a full three hours sleep.

HEARTS AFLAME

The next day I kept thinking about what had happened the

night before. Why was I more interested in my own needs than the eternal destiny of those two ladies? There was a time early in my Christian life when I had that same zeal, the same compassion for non-Christians as did my Eastern European counterparts. What happened? I had plenty of time to think through that question because we spent the next three days in the domestic airport of Moscow waiting for a flight to Siberia. I did some real soul-searching. These guys with whom I was traveling weren't some wild-eyed fanatics. They were young (mid-thirties), articulate, and very intelligent. Titus, a medical doctor, Vladimir, a lawyer, and Vasile, a Baptist youth leader, are part of the new generation of younger Christians that God is raising up to carry the torch of the gospel into the next century in Eastern Europe. Their hearts are aflame with the love of Christ for their fellow countrymen.

"Sammy, I believe the greatest need of Eastern Europe is not sweeping political change . . . [but] a mighty spiritual change in the hearts of men and women."

Titus has been a challenge to my life for many years. We worked together during the dark days of Ceaucescu's evil dictatorship. God had knit our hearts together through struggles, suffering, and the proclaiming of Christ throughout Romania. When the revolution swept Romania, I immediately went there. Titus and I spent many hours discussing his future as well as the future of the country. During the demonstrations that erupted in his home city of Oradea, Titus had spoken about how democracy works; he also spoke about some of the ideas of Francis Schaeffer, a favorite author of his. The crowds cheered for those they wanted to lead them during this transitional period. As a result, Titus was among a group of men asked by the masses to help in a transition. He agreed and for two months Titus headed social welfare.

Five months later elections would take place. Titus asked me repeatedly, "Should I stay in the political arena of life, go back to my medical profession, or minister full time during these days of freedom?"

I told Titus that only God could give him that answer. We spent many hours discussing and praying about what he should do. Before I left the country, he came to the conclusion that he should give his life to full-time ministry. He said, "Sammy, I believe the greatest need of Eastern Europe at this time is not sweeping political change. It's not social or moral change. We need a more fundamental change than all of that. We need to see a mighty spiritual change in the hearts of men and women. Without that basic change of heart, the political, social, and moral changes will only be temporary. Eastern Europe will flounder in chaos and confusion unless there is the fundamental change in the hearts of the people."

What Titus said to me during those days following the revolution was the answer to my question in the airport. Two highly educated young men in Eastern Europe lived with a keen sense of the hopelessness and helplessness that dwelt deeply in the hearts of their people. They understood that society could change for the good only if there was a grass-roots spiritual change in people's hearts, minds, and attitudes. They knew what Christians in the West need to learn. We must win the battle for the hearts of men and women before we will ever win the battle for society.

We've had the tendency in the West to think that we could restore greatness to our nations through political muscle and strength. We've believed that a political leader or party platform could bring us back to the faith and morality of our forefathers. However, we've been disappointed time and time again by the changing directions of political winds. I certainly believe that the Christian community should be involved in every level of the political process. But we must also understand that the West will not change until the hearts of people in the West change.

CHANGING ATTITUDES

Evangelism is at the very center of bringing that change to the hearts of people. Hearts and attitudes change because people come to know Christ. As deep attitudes change, then ultimately society changes. Therefore, the greatest thing we can do to change society is to present people with the claims of Christ. Before I became a Christian, I had deep racial animosity and prejudice. The culture in which I was reared typically taught that black people were not equal to white people. During my junior year of high school, our school was integrated for the first time. Anger and hate filled my heart as well as many of my classmates. The government could force integration of the schools, but it could not change our hearts.

Then a man told me about Jesus. He didn't speak with me about my lousy racial attitudes. He spoke to me about Christ and what He could do in my heart. That night I opened my heart to Christ. He came into my life and began the process of making radical changes. Among other changes, God gave me a new pair of eyes. I no longer saw people in terms of black or white. I simply saw them as people—created in God's image, with a capacity to know Him. There was such a love in my heart for people of other races that I actually thought something was wrong with me. I went to an older Christian and confided in him about my feelings. I was relieved when he told me that Christians were supposed to feel that way. I still consider that as the greatest miracle of God that I have ever experienced—the miracle of a changed heart. When someone asks for proof of the existence of God, I point them to that great change He made in my life more than twenty-eight years ago. I tell them of how He changed a heart of hatred and prejudice into one of love and acceptance.

EVANGELISM AND CHANGE

Even though evangelism is at the very heart of affecting change within society, it has become a derogatory term at the close of the twentieth century. Terms such as *evangelism, evangelist,* and *evangelical* are rapidly falling into disrepute within our Western culture. But even more alarming is the fact that the church itself has begun to look upon the evangelist and evangelism with disdain. I recently spoke at a national-level conference in which I was one of several speakers who were evangelists. However, the others didn't identify themselves as evangelists. They used more creative words, such as *conference speaker* and *youth consultant* to identify themselves. How and why have we developed such a negative and critical view in the West about that which can produce positive change in society?

First, Western civilization no longer identifies itself as Christian. We now claim to be a pluralistic society. Pluralism cannot live peacefully with absolutes. Anyone in a pluralistic society who claims to believe in that which is absolute will be viewed as narrow-minded and nonintellectual. It's OK in a pluralistic society to say that Jesus is a way to God and that you believe in Him. Just don't say that He is "the way, the truth, and the life, and no one comes to the Father but through Him." If you do, you may be branded a bigot. In a pluralistic culture it's all right to speak of the beauty of marriage. Just don't say that adultery and homosexuality are sin. If you do, then you have closed yourself to intellectual thought.

Of course, as evangelical Christians we hold those truths of the Bible as absolutes. Most of us would never compromise on those issues. However, we have very subtly been intimidated by the enemy. We hold fast to the truth of God's Word, but we find ourselves insecure and fearful of being seen as narrow-minded in an age of intellectual pluralism.

In chapter 1, I told the story of the businessman from Holland who was in Norilsk, Siberia, at the same time I was holding a crusade. He became very angry during our discussion about Christianity. He continually attempted to portray Christians as narrow-minded. I found myself trying to defend myself and prove that I was objective in my thinking.

However, I was interrupted by Titus, my Romanian medical doctor friend. Unapologetically he said, "Wait just a moment, Sammy. I would like to say that I am narrow, *very* narrow. I admit that. And, sir"—Titus looked at the man from Western

Europe—"you need to know that the way of Jesus is a very narrow one. And you will never enter His kingdom unless you are willing to place you feet, heart, and soul on that narrow path."

I learned a great lesson that day. I realized how subtly I had become intimidated by pluralistic thought. If you had asked me prior to Titus' comments, I would have denied any feelings of intimidation. But I found myself quick to defend myself rather than present the claims of Christ. Pluralism pervades our culture. To a great extent Western Christians have apologetically blended into the background of the culture. With fear in our hearts we have ceased presenting absolute truth that can cure the spiritual cancer that has so affected our society.

The second reason that evangelism has fallen on hard times is because of a mistaken understanding of its nature. Both within and without the church, an erroneous view has grown up about the evangelist and the nature of evangelism. Recently American moviegoers watched a film entitled *A Leap Of Faith*. The advertisements said that it was a story about an evangelist who was a swindler and phony. I normally wouldn't waste money to go see such a movie. Because it was portraying an evangelist, I wanted to see what kind of propaganda the public was being fed about the ministry of evangelism and the evangelist. I wanted to know what people were being told to think about people like me, because I unashamedly admit that I am involved in the work of evangelism.

My wife and I wept as we watched the movie, not just because it portrayed the main character as a shyster. We wept because the world was being given a completely wrong description of what an evangelist really is. In the movie the corrupt minister "slays people in the spirit" and heals them "in the name of Jesus." All of that has absolutely *nothing* to do with evangelism. Where did the world get such an idea about evangelism? Unfortunately, from the church.

The star of the movie said that he watched Benny Hinn to know how to play the part of "slaying people in the spirit." I've watched Benny Hinn on television. Without commenting on the effectiveness of what Hinn does, I can say one thing he does not do—the work of evangelism! Evangelism isn't zapping people so that they fall over in some trance-like state. It's not praying over them so that they will be healed. It's simply and clearly telling people that they are separated from a holy God by their sins. It's telling them of what Jesus has done to forgive them and cleanse them from their sin and bring them back to God. The world has become confused about evangelism and the evangelist because the church is confused.

As I have traveled in Africa and South America, I've found many Christians very skeptical about the ministry of evangelism. That skepticism has grown from a host of people from Western Europe and North America who call themselves evangelists. They come in and announce that they will pray for the sick. They fill stadiums with multitudes suffering from all sorts of diseases. They pray for God to "heal them" and they "cast out demons." Many pastors and missionaries (including charismatic and Pentecostal pastors) have told me that when the meetings have concluded they have a hard time finding any lasting fruit. There's good reason for that. Casting out demons, healings, or "signs and wonders" is not evangelism. The power of God in healing is not evangelism. Evangelism is the power of the cross, of a sacrifice that restores us to God. It's the story of God's love and man's sin, bridged by a cruel cross where Jesus, God's Son, suffered the penalty and brought us back to God. I'm not saying that God doesn't heal people today or that people can't be possessed by evil spirits. I'm simply saying that those things must not be confused with evangelism.

Evangelism is not Christian entertainment. An entire entertainment industry has grown up in the evangelical church in recent years. *Televangelism* and *televangelist* have become common terms. I must admit that I don't watch much Christian television. But I have only seen one person on television whom I believe does the work of evangelism—Billy Graham. That's not to say that there aren't others. But what I have seen is Christian entertainment, Christian instruction, faith healers, and a host of other things—but not evangelism. Evangelism has gotten a bad rap in the church because we don't understand what it is. A whole lot of religious activity has been put under the umbrella of evangelism. I believe that Satan has attempted to distort the work of evangelism because it is that which places the church on the cutting edge of piercing the darkness.

A final reason that evangelism has become difficult in the West is the well-publicized fall of nationally and internationally known evangelists. Not long after Jimmy Swaggart's first scandal was made public, I was having breakfast with a Christian friend I'll call James. One of James's acquaintances came into the restaurant, and James invited him to have breakfast with us. He introduced me to the gentleman as an international evangelist. The man began to laugh and said, "Well, I guess business is bad for you!"

James's acquaintance was mistaken on several counts. First, I'm not in business. Second, Swaggart and I are not in the same category. I don't live in a mansion and don't visit prostitutes. But what the man said was important. There's a general perception today that anyone involved in evangelism must have some big sex problems or an ulterior motive for what he is doing. I know a lot of evangelists. Most of them are dirt poor and struggle for survival. They do what they do because they love God and they love people.

EVANGELISM AND YOU

We must not allow the devil to dirty that which God declares holy. We must regain a healthy understanding and respect for evangelism. It's the first step toward piercing the darkness, and each of us is to be involved in it. Remember, the Great Commission Jesus gave to all His disciples was to "go into the world and make disciples." All of us are involved; we all are evangelists, even though we may not all be called to serve God as full-time evangelists.

The key reason that Satan has tried to muddy the waters of evangelism lies in that fact that every Christian is to be involved in the ministry of evangelism. Satan has attempted to confuse the church and leave it impotent in piercing the darkness. Within the heart of every true Christian lies the hope for such a needy world. If Christ has changed our lives, then we have light within us. We must allow that light to shine brightly in and through us to touch those around us. Someone has rightly defined the work of evangelism as "one beggar telling another beggar where to find the bread of life."

Some Christians may think, "Sammy, you're an evangelist. All of this is OK for you, but not me. I'm just an ordinary Christian. There's nothing special about me. I agree that we need to understand the work of evangelism and regain a healthy respect for that ministry. So, I'll pray for you and others like you. But I don't believe that I could or should do the work of evangelism."

It's true that not everyone can or should minister in a full-time capacity as an evangelist. God calls certain individuals and gifts them as evangelists. And then He gives those individuals to the church (Ephesians 4:11–12). But every Christian has been given a responsibility to reach others for Christ, which is the ministry of evangelism. Paul said that everyone who is in Christ has received a new heart and new life (2 Corinthians 5:17). He then says, "Now all these things are from God, who reconciled us to Himself through Christ, and gave us the ministry of reconciliation" (verse 18). If our darkened hearts have been pierced by the light of the gospel, then we must not hold that light within us. We must allow it to shine through us to others who desperately need to know Christ.

The only qualification to be used of God to see others' hearts changed is to know that your heart has been changed by God. When Tex and I were first married, I served as interim pastor of the Jerusalem Baptist Church in Pumpkin Center, Louisiana. In that rural community of south Louisiana, common, ordinary people cared and had an impact. Consider Jerry, a foster child raised by a deacon of the church. Jerry had suffered much abuse and neglect and now had a very bad stuttering problem. But this Christian family exemplified the love of Jesus to Jerry. One Sunday at the conclusion of my message, Jerry came to me and said, "I need God. I want to have Christ in my heart."

We prayed together that morning, and Jerry opened his heart to Jesus. The love of God began a wonderful healing process in his heart. When Jerry would ride the bus to school, some of the boys would make fun of him because of his stuttering. Sometimes they would hit him. After his experience with Christ, he would say to them, "D—d—don't do that. J—J—J—Jesus loves you. He's in m—m—my heart." It took him a while to get it all out. But one by one he told all the boys about Christ. Every week Jerry would have a new friend with him in church. I baptized more people that Jerry brought to Christ than any other person in our congregation brought. Jerry was greatly used of God, not because he had great talents and speaking abilities. The darkness in his heart had been pierced by the light of God's love. He was simply "one beggar telling another beggar where to find the bread of life."

As darkness quickly covers the Western world, we desperately need common, ordinary people like Jerry. We need men and women whose darkened hearts have been changed by the light of God's love. And we must penetrate our dark world with the message that Christ is our only hope.

Before our gospelizing gets around to the uttermost part of the earth, it should begin at home, "in Jerusalem" as it were. We have a story to tell to the nations, but it is also a story to tell to the neighbors all around us.

Vance Havner
The Vance Havner Quotebook

And pray on my behalf, that utterance may be given to me in the opening of my mouth, to make known with boldness the mystery of the gospel, for which I am an ambassador in chains; that in proclaiming it I may speak boldly, as I ought to speak.

Ephesians 6:19–20

11

Developing
Relationships

I wondered how they came to know Christ, when missionary efforts had been outlawed so long. Yet here I sat in the restaurant of the Ulan Bator hotel enjoying the fellowship of Mongolian Christian friends. The gospel had been forbidden by Buddhists rulers for nearly 2,000 years. Then the communists took over the country, and they refused to allow any faith to flourish. Christian Scriptures translated into the Mongolian language did not even exist until the last year and a half prior to our meeting. When we finally did meet, the Mongolians had only the New Testament in their language.

I asked these leaders of Mongolia's small Christian community to explain how they first heard about Christ. Their stories were fascinating. One of them said, "I was a student at the university in Moscow. My roommate was from Tanzania. Every night before he went to sleep, He would pull the covers over his head and take out a small book. He would then turn on a flashlight and read for a half hour. He did this for a year. Finally, I asked him what he was reading. It was then that he told me about the Bible and about Jesus. I returned to our country, and freedom began to emerge in our nation. I met a man from the United States. He came here and told me more about Jesus, and I became a follower of Christ."

Another young Mongolian spoke up. "I was a student in the university in Leipzig, East Germany. A Lutheran pastor befriended me and began to tell me about Jesus. After a long time of hearing and learning about Him, I became a believer. I gave my heart to Christ in East Germany. But I didn't think that there were any Christians in Mongolia. When I returned not too long ago, I met these friends. I am so excited to be a part of the beginning of bringing Christianity to my people."

I was overcome by the goodness and greatness of our God. He used an evil system opposed to Christianity to open a nation to the gospel. In the communists' zeal to bring their ideology to the whole world, they brought students from Mongolia to a university that propagated atheism. Amazingly at those communist universities they first heard of the Savior. I was again reminded of the sovereignty of God. No matter how dark the world looks, He is still on the throne. Communists and atheists cannot stop Him. He still orders the events of human history. His purposes will be accomplished.

But I also realized that Christians have a great responsibility placed on their shoulders. When God gets ready to work in the hearts of people, many times He brings Christians across their paths at a strategic moment in their lives. As Christians develop relationships with the non-Christians, opportunities arise to bring the great message of God's salvation. I'm sure that the Tanzanian and the German could never have imagined the far-reaching results that their relationships with these men would produce.

When we think of piercing the darkness, we often think of the great heroes of the faith. We think of men and women who left everything to become missionaries. Or we think of the great evangelists, and we say, "They are the ones who can impact our world for Christ. I will pray for them and support them. But I could never do that." Yet, God often uses the most humble of persons to accomplish great things in the local setting. He will take a university student from a poor African nation or a pastor of a small church in a closed country and use them.

Recently, I spoke at a national conference in the United States about the needs of the world and the need to broaden our vision. At the close of the meeting, a group from New York City asked me, "How can we have a vision for the world when we are overwhelmed with New York City? There are millions in our own city. How can we think beyond that which is already much bigger than us?"

"I know that your task is a great one," I said. "But you must understand that you don't have to go very far to reach the world. The world is in New York City. There are communities of almost every nationality in the world right in your city. Many of those living there will be much more open to the gospel in New York than they would be in their own home countries. If you can develop relationships with some of those from other countries, you could ultimately reach the whole world and never have to leave New York."

OUR NEIGHBORS, OUR WORLD

What I said to those young adults stands true for North American and Western European Christians. Today communication and transportation have made the world a very small place. Communication satellites let us see into Moscow's Red Square instantly. Jet travel whisks us from Los Angeles to the Philippines in fourteen hours. And many people from other lands have become immigrants living in the West. If Christians would learn to develop Christ-honoring relationships with non-Christians in their own neighborhoods, our light would begin to penetrate the darkest areas of our society. We could all become world missionaries right where we live through simple relationships.

Recently, I visited my mother in the hospital in Louisiana. Janet (not her real name), a friend of my mother, was also visiting, and she told me about how God had used her to lead to Christ a Buddhist lady from Japan. How did this lady from Louisiana help this woman from Japan meet the Savior?

During a previous evangelistic meeting in Louisiana, I mentioned the just-completed crusades in Moldavia. I told the crowd of a peasant woman who came to the platform all by herself. Eventually Janet heard me share the testimony.

Later, Janet was at a luncheon meeting with other Christian women. She was telling them the story of the peasant woman when she noticed the Japanese waitress standing nearby listening. She looked more closely and saw tears in her eyes. She befriended the waitress and discovered that she had just recently moved from Japan to the States. She was from a Buddhist background. Their friendship developed, and Janet eventually led the lady to Christ. She said to me that day in the hospital, "Sammy, this lady is really growing in Christ and is on fire for the Lord."

I'm convinced that there are many people in our communities who are ready to receive the gospel. They just need someone who has built "a platform" from which to speak to them. That platform most often is a credible relationship that makes the gospel believable. Sometimes that platform takes years to build; sometimes only a few moments. When we become believable, then the gospel becomes understandable. It doesn't take great talent to make the gospel understandable. It only takes the right kind of living and the right kind of relationships. With those two tools, we build the platform from which to speak about Christ. We can then be easily understood. But from a practical viewpoint, how do we build those relationships?

THE ROLE OF PRAYER

It begins with prayer. We must see people through the eyes of Christ's love and compassion. Prayer enables us to do that. I had the opportunity to lead some prayer seminars in Scotland in preparation for Billy Graham's "Mission Scotland." It was a great learning experience for me. As a younger evangelist I wanted to learn all that I could about the man and his organization that has been so mightily used of the Lord to bring millions to Christ. Although I didn't have the opportunity to meet Dr. Graham, I was especially impressed with two things I saw and heard in those preparation meetings.

First, the director of the crusade made an important observation. He said, "Mass evangelism is really personal evangelism done in a massive way." That rang a bell with me. Any massive evangelistic effort that's not rooted in an emphasis on personal evangelism will never reach its full potential of penetrating the darkness. In the battle for the hearts and minds of men and women, it will take every individual believer reaching out to those trapped in darkness. Any great evangelistic harvest must be a grassroots people-to-people movement if lasting results are to be experienced.

Second, the primary method through which Christians in Scotland were mobilized to reach the nation was prayer. Everyone was encouraged to make a list of five people for whom they were going to pray. They were encouraged not only to pray for their relatives, friends, and colleagues, but also to invite them to hear Billy Graham speak. One night at the City Halls Auditorium in Glasgow, I gave instructions to the Christians in attendance to make their list of five people and pray for them. A lady came to me at the close of the meeting and said, "Mr. Tippit, I made my list a week ago. And this lady with me is the first person on my list. She is my neighbor. Last night she gave her heart to Christ."

It was thrilling to hear that dear lady's testimony. It didn't take Billy Graham arriving in Glasgow for people to come to Christ. It took people coming under God's burden to pray for those with whom they already had established relationships. They then began to reach out to those people. I returned to Glasgow several months after Dr. Graham's mission and heard moving reports of God in action through His people. The mission coordinator said that several hundred people came to Christ before Graham ever set his feet on Scottish soil. Yes, Graham was used mightily of God. But perhaps one of the greatest things he did in Scotland was to mobilize the Christian community to begin to pray for their friends, relatives, and colleagues.

Many of the great revivals of history have had the same emphasis. The great awakening in Northern Ireland that I mentioned previously began with four Bible study teachers. They began praying for individuals specifically who didn't know Christ. As people begin to come to know Christ, the word spread throughout the community about God answering prayer. And the fires of revival were lit. When God began to move in Romania twenty years ago, it began with a faithful pastor who taught the people to pray. He taught them to pray specifically for friends, colleagues, relatives, atheists, and persecutors. One by one, God answered their prayers until the fires of revival were released upon the nation.

This simple method of people praying for people is crucial, and it is the primary focus in our crusades around the world. Before I will travel to a nation to preach an evangelistic crusade, I first go into that country and set the Christians to praying. Lots of money and extraordinary amounts of publicity cannot produce the kind of lasting fruit that comes from people praying for people.

Effective Prayers

Allow me to offer some suggestions about how we can pray. First, pray for those with whom you already have a relationship. They may never be burdened about their own salvation unless you first become burdened about their salvation. They may be comfortable with the darkness and see no need for God. But prayer has a way of shaking them out of their comfort zones. I know a man whose mother told him that she wasn't a Christian and never would become one. She refused to let him speak to her about God. So, he spoke to God about her. After twenty years of praying, his mother called him one day on the phone and said, "I need God!" Twenty years of praying forced her out of her comfort zone and into the position of need. Then God could work in her life.

Pray for those with whom you have relationships in several ways. *Pray specifically*. Don't pray in vague generalities for "all those who don't know Christ." Pray specifically and watch God answer specifically. *Pray persistently*. Don't give up. Don't lose hope. The man I mentioned previously prayed for over twenty years. Too many Christians pray "instant prayers" and expect "instant answers." We must learn to persist in prayer and not give up. *Pray passionately*. I'm afraid that many Christians in the West have lost their ability to weep for the lost. We seem to be afraid of emotion. I would agree that emotionalism is unhealthy. When we begin to live by emotions rather than the truth of God's Word, it can always be dangerous. However, weeping over someone's eternal destiny is not emotionalism. It's simply coming face-to-face with the truth of what God's Word says about the condition of the human heart outside of Christ.

Fear is probably the greatest hindrance to our being able to shatter the darkness. We fear failure, rejection, and what others will think about or do to us.

Second, pray that God would give you courage to share Christ with those with whom you have a relationship. As you begin to pray for your non-Christian acquaintances, God will begin to work in their hearts. He will prepare circumstances in their lives that will cause them to be receptive to the gospel. Many times people are wanting to know how to know Christ. We just haven't had the courage to tell them of God's love. Fear is probably the greatest hindrance to our being able to shatter the darkness. We fear failure, rejection, and what others will think about or do to us. Many Christians have become slaves to fear. But Paul said, "God has not given us a spirit of timidity, but of power, love, and discipline" (2 Timothy 1:7). When he wrote about spiritual warfare, he concluded by asking others to pray for him that he would have courage to tell everyone with whom he was related about the wonderful love of Jesus. He was in chains, a prisoner. But he saw the opportunity to tell even the guards about Jesus. He just needed courage to pierce the darkness. Ask God to give you courage to tell others the good things that God has done for you.

Finally, pray that God will enable you to build new relationships with non-Christians in order to share Christ with them. This action probably is the most difficult to take. The longer that we walk with the Lord, the more difficult it becomes to relate to non-Christians. In a certain sense, that's the way it should be. Our deepest and most intimate relationships should be with those who have the same commitment to Christ that we have to Him. However, if we're not careful our relationships can become no more than "holy huddles." We can become comfortable with "good Christian fellowship." Futhermore, as darkness covers Western civilization, we may prefer to retreat to the safety of our Christian comfort zones.

A few years ago my wife and I were invited to a high society function in our city. I really didn't want to go because I didn't think that I would be very comfortable with that setting. We prayed about it and felt that God would have us go. We asked God to somehow allow us to develop a relationship with someone who needed Him and was open to the message of Christ.

When we arrived, we were escorted to our table. We sat there with people whom we had never met and with whom we thought we had absolutely nothing in common. After a while we struck up a conversation with another couple at the table. We were surprised when we discovered the background of this couple. They were Ukrainian Jews who had just immigrated to the United States. I told them that I had just returned from Kishinev, Moldavia. They were very excited about that because they had friends near Kishinev. They asked me what I was doing in Kishinev. I explained that I was a Christian evangelist and that I traveled internationally.

I expected that they would react negatively when I told them about myself. But they responded in the opposite fashion. The lady said, "Oh, this is very unusual. The man from whom we buy our insurance was by our house this week. He told us that he also is Jewish. But he told us that he believes in Jesus as the Messiah. He told us that he would pray for us that we would come to know Jesus as the Messiah. He also said that he would pray that we would meet other believers who would be able to explain to us about the Messiah. We are very interested in this."

That couple didn't come to know Christ that evening. But God opened a door and began a relationship at that time. Only eternity will tell the final results of that meeting. It would have been easy to stay in the confines of our Christian comfort zone. But God had a different idea of how we should spend our evening. We were looking forward to a nice lazy, relaxing evening. But God knew there was a battle taking place for the hearts of two Jewish immigrants from the Ukraine.

Jesus continually went to the unthinkable places. . . . His light turned the ugliest hearts into the most beautiful ones.

If every Christian would simply explain Christ's love to those with whom they already have a relationship, revival would spread throughout our communities. If we would begin to pray and ask God to help us establish relationships with those who need Him and are seeking Him, then I believe that the darkness would begin to dissipate. The first step is to take the light to the nearest concentration of darkness.

Jesus continually went to the unthinkable places. He never allowed His light to be hidden behind stained glass windows. He didn't pierce the darkness by basking in the sunshine. He found sinners with the darkest of hearts. His light turned the ugliest hearts into the most beautiful ones. Paul continually sought to meet people where they lived and worked. He didn't ask them to come to him. He went to them. And he let his light shine.

Those who have gone before us, both in the Bible and throughout history, have been those who refused to stay in their comfort zones. They went straight to the frontlines of the battle. With the Word of God, the love of His Son, and the saving light of the gospel, they invaded the darkness. They established relationships. They built a platform from which to speak. They prayed. And the darkness was shattered by the Light!

Let God send the fire of His Spirit here, and the minister will be more and more lost in his Master. You will come to think less of the speaker and more of the truth spoken. . . .

Suppose the fire should come here, and the Master be seen more than the minister, what then? Why, this church will become two, three and four thousand strong. . . . We shall have the lecture hall beneath this platform crowded at each prayer meeting, and we shall see in this place young men devoting themselves to God; we shall find ministers raised up, and trained, and sent forth to carry the fire to other parts of the globe. . . . If God shall bless us, He will make us a blessing to multitudes of others.

Let God but send down the fire, and the biggest sinners in the neighborhood will be converted; those who live in dens of infamy will be changed; the drunkard will forsake his cups, the swearer will repent of his blasphemy, the debauched will leave their lusts—dry bones be raised, and clothed afresh, and hearts of stone be turned to flesh."[1]

Charles H. Spurgeon
First sermon in the
Metropolitan Tabernacle,
March 31, 1861

Go therefore and make disciples of all the nations, baptizing them in the name of the Father, and the Son and the Holy Spirit, teaching them to observe all that I commanded you; and lo, I am with you always, even to the end of the age.

Matthew 28:19–20

12

A Balanced
Attack

It was my first day in Albania, and I was excited to be in this former Communist country, a country unlike its Eastern European neighbors for several reasons. First, Albania was the only nation officially declared as "atheist" during the dark days of communism in Europe. Second, it was the most isolated communist country in Eastern Europe, refusing to join the Warsaw Pact. Therefore, it was not aligned with the Soviet Union. Today it remains the poorest nation in Europe.

But in its religious history lay one of the greatest differences between Albania and other Eastern European nations. Most Eastern Europeans trace their spiritual and religious roots back to Christianity. In contrast, 70 percent of present-day Albanians claim a Muslim heritage. Therefore, I knew that Albania would be different from many of the places in which I have ministered. Our strategy needed to be a thorough one that could truly meet the needs of the people.

During this first trip into Albania we would try to discern how to best reach the spiritual needs of the nation. Our team met with a missionary for a meal that first evening. I wanted to learn all that I could on this first visit to the nation. We felt like rookies, for the nation had opened to the gospel message only in the past couple years. This missionary, though, had great insight into how to reach Albanians with the gospel. At one point he said, "A lot of Western Christians come here with a desire to evangelize. But they don't understand that evangelism is only half of the task. Evangelism is like an arrowhead. The point of the arrowhead is evangelism. But that's insufficient to inflict damage on the enemy. The rest of the arrowhead is discipleship. The entire arrowhead is needed to defeat the forces of darkness within Albania."

I thought about his illustration. The arrowhead approach is valid for more than the people of Albania. It can work in every situation in which Christians have been given the task of piercing the darkness. Unfortunately many Christians attempt to fight the enemy with a broken arrowhead. Some take only the point of the arrowhead and attack the enemy. But the broken tip of an arrowhead can hardly wound the enemy; the only thing that can be done with the tip is prick the enemy. That really doesn't harm the enemy. It merely stirs him up.

For many other Christians, the approach is to use the rest of the arrowhead but ignore the tip. They love to disciple other Christians, but they never involve themselves in penetrating enemy territory. However, an arrowhead without a sharpened tip can't harm the enemy either. It can be polished and put in a museum for display. But it will never be able to destroy the works of Satan in the human heart. We have too many churches that have become museums where we show off our well-polished arrowheads. We measure our discipleship by attendance, giving, and the beauty of sanctuaries. But we do not present the gospel; we avoid evangelism. We indulge ourselves in displaying the shining arrowheads of discipleship even as darkness continues, impervious to the dull points of the arrowheads.

THE NEED TO DISCIPLE

Though an arrowhead is useless when the tip has been broken off, it also is wasted when the rest of the head is ill-formed. It was created to be shot in its entirety, evangelistic tip and discipling body. Evangelism and discipleship cannot be separated if we are to dispel the darkness with the light of God's Word.

The reason that discipleship is so vital to evangelism is because it is the method through which God produces men and women of character. Discipleship places people on the road to Christlike character. As new Christians are born into the kingdom of God, they must be enabled to grow into effective witnesses for Christ. As that process takes place, evangelism takes on an entirely new dimension—spiritual multiplication. However, discipleship without evangelism will always lead to comfortable Christianity where believers become spiritually fat and lazy.

Much of the modern discipleship movement has been robbed of its tremendous potential. Many of those committed to discipleship have become content with teaching others the great truths of the Christian life. They often teach others how to go deeper in the things of God, but they have forgotten to look outward among those who are hurting and without Christ. Discipleship without evangelism won't pierce the darkness any more than evangelism without discipleship. Evangelism is the proclamation of all that Christ has done in order to make us right with God. Discipleship is the road upon which the new believer embarks as he decides to place his faith in Jesus. Evangelism looks out upon the harvest. Discipleship looks into the deep parts of the heart. Both are needed and can fulfill their potential in the kingdom of God only as they work with one another.

The key to understanding how to effectively penetrate the darkness is in spiritual balance. Jesus was the most balanced human being who ever lived. He was full of grace and yet altogether just. He was absolute purity but full of mercy. Every attribute of His was balanced by a differing character quality. But He wasn't just balanced in His personhood; he was also balanced in His method and approach to ministering to others. He preached to the multitudes, but he poured His life into twelve men. He always reached out to those who were hurting and lonely. But He spent intimate time training those who would become the fathers of the Christian movement. He was altogether God, and yet completely man. He was the king but also the servant. To learn of Jesus is to learn balance. C. E. Autrey, former professor of evangelism at Southwestern Baptist Theological Seminary, has identified five biblical words used to describe evangelism in his book *Basic Evangelism*. They identify a balanced approach to reaching the world.

> 1) The word *euaggelidzo* in the Greek means, "I preach glad tidings." It is our word for "gospel." The verb form of the word means to gospelize. . . . 2) The word *karuso* was used in connection with John, Jesus, and the early disciples . . . . *Karuso* means, "to herald." 3) *Didasko* is used more often than any other word in describing the evangelism of Jesus. "Jesus went about all the cities and villages, teaching in their synagogues" (Matthew 9:35). 4) The fourth word which must be considered is the word *martus*, "witness." From the word *witness*, we get our word "martyr." A martyr is one who backs up his testimony with his blood. A genuine New Testament witness will preach the Gospel and will die for it, also. 5) The last word which elucidates the Biblical definition of evangelism is *mathatas*, "disciple." *Mathateusate* is the verb form used here (Matt. 28:19). It is the word "disciple." It means more than leading a man to become a Christian. It means to instruct him, also. It means to make him a learner, a student. It means to fulfill all that is embraced in discipling.[2]

FOUR TYPES OF EVANGELISM

Jesus used a balanced approach to overthrow evil. He employed every method to transform hearts and set captive lives free. We must understand that His work is balanced and complete. At the very center of His method was personal evangelism. He was the great personal evangelist because He knew that the kingdom of God would be built one heart at a time. Let me offer a strategy that I believe will produce a balanced attack on the forces of evil in this day.

Discipleship Evangelism

Discipleship evangelism has two aspects, both useful for penetrating the darkness. First, it involves discipling men and women to present the gospel. Second, those disciples learn to disciple others who accept the gospel, so the new converts can reproduce the process. This two-step process results in spiritual multiplication. The Bible speaks of many being "added unto the church." But there came a point in the book of Acts where the principle of addition was overtaken by the principle of multiplication. Those who came to know Christ shared their faith in Jesus with those around them. When they came to Christ, they were taught the Word of God until they also led others to faith in Christ. Consequently, the word multiplied.

When I pastored in Germany, I quickly became discouraged because only one or two members in the church seemed interested in declaring the love of Jesus to the non-Christians around them. I started discipling some men, and my wife started discipling some women. We taught them how to walk with God and present their faith to others. One by one those men and women became strong witnesses of Christ. Each of them began to lead others to Christ.

One of the men was John Labash, the hospital administrator at the American air force base. As he grew in the Word of God, he became concerned for his boss, the commander of the hospital. John and his wife, Betty, began slowly explaining God's impact on their lives to Spencer Downs and his wife. Dr. Downs and Corky came to one of our Sunday evening worship services. The first thing he said to me when we met was, "I don't have any purpose in life." It wasn't long afterward that John and Betty helped lead Dr. Downs and Corky to Christ. The Downses began to grow in Christ, and they began to lead family members and friends to Christ. Dr. Downs eventually became the surgeon general of the Air National Guard of the United States. He later retired from the military and attended Dallas Theological Seminary. At the time he was the oldest student enrolled. Presently he is serving in a pastoral ministry in Indiana. This story of spiritual multiplication was reproduced numerous times through discipleship at that air base in Germany. Our church experienced phenomenal growth—not because of population shifts but because we discovered the power of discipleship evangelism.

For maximum effectiveness, discipleship evangelism requires two things: to *impart the Word of God* into the hearts of the disciples and to *impart our very own lives.* Clearly we must teach others the Word of God. Without the Bible people will never penetrate the darkness. The psalmist said, "Thy word is a lamp to my feet, and a light to my path" (Psalm 119:105). We must make disciples who are able to penetrate the darkness with the light of God's Word. But we must also impart our very own heartbeat to others. This is probably the most difficult part of discipleship evangelism.

Deep within the heart of every person is a desire to know God. It's one of the great proofs of the existence of God.

If we don't have a passion to lead others to Christ, then those we are discipling probably will not have passion either. If our tears are dry, then we can't expect that those we are discipling will cry to God for their non-Christian friends. We produce hearts like our own. If our hearts are on fire to bring others to Christ, then we will find that fire will spread rapidly to those we are discipling. We must be open and transparent if we are to make disciples who will have a heart to win the spiritual battle. Paul said, "For our gospel did not come to you in word only, but also in power and in the Holy Spirit and with full conviction; just as you know what kind of men we proved to be among you for your sake" (1 Thessalonians 1:5). Paul and his "rag tag" band of disciples shook the entire Roman Empire. They caught his genuineness and his fire. It wasn't difficult for that fire to spread rapidly among those who walked with him.

Direct evangelism

As a method of reaching men and women for Christ, direct evangelism has fallen into disrepute in the last several years. Many Christian groups even question whether it is a valid expression of outreach at the close of the twentieth century. Some have already held funeral services for such an approach to winning the battle for the hearts and minds of this generation. I strongly disagree for one primary reason. Deep within the heart of every person is a desire to know God. That's a fact about every person in every culture and every generation. It's one of the great proofs of the existence of God.

Long before communism collapsed in Eastern Europe, I preached and witnessed openly and directly throughout Eastern Europe. People constantly told me, "You can't do that. It's not permitted. The people have been brainwashed against Christianity." One well-known leader told me only to get Bibles to the Christians. He said that would be the extent of what anyone would be able to accomplish. However, I had a deep conviction that all people were created in God's image. Consequently, I knew that there was a longing in Eastern Europeans to know their Creator.

Sixteen years before the collapse of communism, two friends and I infiltrated a Communist youth world festival in East Berlin. Over 100,000 hard-core Communist young people were coming to the fest to be trained to evangelize the world for communism and atheism. God placed a deep burden on Fred Bishop, Fred Starkweather, and me to share the gospel with those communist youth. An old Lutheran pastor said to me, "Sammy, you must come. This will be a once-in-a-lifetime opportunity to reach these young people." I must admit that at first I was somewhat concerned. These weren't the typical Eastern European teenagers. These were hard-core communist kids.

The first night of the fest we were surprised when young people began to ask us for our autographs. We were obviously from the West and they wanted the autographs of foreigners. We obliged them and also began sharing the gospel. I was overwhelmed with the response. Yes, there was a good bit of rejection. But most of all we found spiritually hungry (or should I say starved) young people at that fest. Almost two hundred communist youths gave their hearts to Christ during the following week.

Our ministry began in Eastern Europe as a result of that direct evangelistic effort. We began traveling to the different cities in Eastern Europe where the new converts lived. We discovered that 95 percent of those young people followed through with their commitment to Christ and became involved in local churches. As a result, we were invited to speak in churches throughout Eastern Europe.

I learned a great lesson through that atheistic youth festival. There is a longing in the heart of every human being to know the God who created him. That longing will always be there no matter how dark the days become. The darker the days, the more intense the search for God will become. I'm afraid that many in the West have been intimidated by the darkness in our society. We've backed off of any direct form of evangelism. We must become courageous for Christ. Along with courage, the church needs to develop three other characteristics as part of direct evangelism: genuine love for people, courtesy in our presentation, and sensitivity to the needs and questions of the nonbelievers.

One U. S. pastor friend has a great philosophy: in every community there are at least six people ready to receive Christ at any moment. "The responsibility of the church is to find those six people," he says. He has begun several churches using that philosophy. I believe he's right. The more open and blatant society becomes with sin, the emptier the hearts of the people become. Jesus came to "seek and save the lost." Our responsibility in these dark days is finding those who are lost, empty, and searching for God. There are many who are ready to receive the gospel. We just need to find them and present the gospel to them.

Indirect Evangelism

The darker the days become, the more hurting people we will find. Many of them will not be open to a direct approach of proclaiming the gospel. Their sole concern will be that of having their needs met. Therefore, we will have to learn to present the gospel in the context of meeting needs. That approach is altogether appropriate. Jesus Himself continually met people at the point of their need. He ministered to their needs and then told them of His forgiveness and salvation. To bring about lasting change within society and the hearts of people, we must learn to become servants to people. This is the essence of indirect evangelism.

Several years ago I spoke at a Florida Christian college and was surrounded by Christians the entire week. I spoke in classes filled with Christians. I lunched with Christian professors. Everything I did was related to believers. When I left to fly back home, I asked God to allow me to share Christ with someone who needed Him. I wanted to break out of the comfort of Christian fellowship. My entire week had been spent talking about penetrating the darkness, but I never really came close to the darkness. It's easy to fall into the trap of becoming an expert on the battle but never engaging in the battle.

When I boarded the plane, I began looking for my seat that had been assigned. I found a screaming baby sitting in it next to her mother. I said, "Excuse me, ma'am, but I believe that this is my seat." The lady apologetically took the baby, and the infant screamed even louder. The crying became worse as the plane took off. I must confess that I sat there complaining to myself, "I wanted to have a deep conversation with someone about Christ. But now I'm stuck next to this screaming baby."

About that time God began to speak to my heart. I began to wonder, *What would Jesus do if He was here?* At that moment the Holy Spirit convicted me. Jesus was there. He was living in me through the person of the Holy Spirit. I silently confessed my failure to Him and asked Him to give me the right attitude. I then looked at the lady and said, "Could I help you with your baby? Could I play with him?"

Immediately she handed the baby and said, "Please!"

After a few minutes of playing with the baby, he fell asleep. The lady began to thank me for the assistance and eventually asked who I was and what I did. As I began explaining the gospel, I noticed tears in her eyes. She said, "I'm not a Christian, but a few weeks ago my husband's mother told us that she had become a Christian. We had many questions that she couldn't answer because she was so new in her faith. And she said to us that she would pray that God would send someone across our paths that could explain to us what it meant to be a Christian."

Evangelism and serving others are not opposed to one another. They should work hand in hand.

I couldn't believe it. It was one of those divine appointments. Yet, I could have easily missed a great opportunity to share Christ with a lady searching for the truth because of my insensitivity. Many people are open to the gospel, but they have immediate needs. If we will learn to meet those needs, we will have very natural opportunities to present the gospel to them.

Missionaries have utilized this method of evangelism for decades. Many nations have been closed to the gospel, but missionaries have often cracked the door by meeting a felt need. There are innumerable needs in Western society. We can be involved in social ministry, educational ministry, and many other forms of service to people. Evangelism and serving others are not opposed to one another. They should work hand in hand.

The pastor who followed me at the church in Germany was one of the men whom I had discipled. The church continued to grow under Don's ministry, and he was greatly used of God. But Don was associated with the military, as the church primarily served the large U.S. air force base there. He eventually left Germany because that air base was selected for closing once the U.S. government began to reduce troop levels in Germany. As American military families moved out of the community, refugees from other parts of the world moved into it, many of them from Eastern Europe.

The refugees came with little more than the clothes on their backs. The church decided to reach out to these needy people. Even as Pastor Don prepared to leave, members began to bring everything from blankets to furniture to their new neighbors. As they expressed Christlike kindness to them, the Christians had many opportunities to present the gospel. By the time the base had completely closed, the church had reached Russians, Croats, and several other nationalities. They formed Bible study groups in homes of the various ethnic groups. They trained ethnic leaders to lead them. On Sunday everyone met together and worshiped in German, and during the week they held Bible studies in their own languages.

That church could have closed and become history. But instead it had a vision and a heart of compassion. It resulted in the darkness being penetrated rather than the death of a church.

Revival Evangelism

Revival evangelism. The two words seem polarized among most evangelical Christians in the West. Those who speak of the need for revival emphasize that the church needs to go deeper with God. Those who promote evangelism proclaim that the church needs to reach outward, not inward. Yet the greatest evangelistic harvests in church history have come during times of revival. Revival of the church and evangelism were not opposed to one another throughout the history of the church. They were two sides of the same coin. They were inseparable. Revival in the church sparked evangelism, and evangelism enlarged the circle of revival.

Revival evangelism is simply the church proclaiming the gospel with a renewed authority and boldness because she has awakened from spiritual slumber and apathy. It is the Holy Spirit reaching out to a lost and hurting world through God's people, who have been renewed. Revival evangelism comes from the deep work of the Holy Spirit in the hearts of Christians. It is outreach that is the result of the overflow of a renewed walk with God.

Revive Us Again

The recent events of Eastern Europe can only be described as God intervening in the affairs of human history. Baptist leaders in Romania recently have told me that nine hundred new Baptist churches have started since the revolution. That doesn't count the other denominations and other nations. During a recent pastors' conference in Moldavia, I conferred with several pastors from the Ukraine where I held crusades. They told me of new churches starting as a result of our crusades. We have seen churches formed in areas of Siberia where Christianity had been nonexistent. None of this can be attributed to some grand strategy or some great organization.

No human personality can take credit for these things. They are a divine act of God. When the Spirit of God moves, souls are converted, and nations are transformed. The darkness is shattered, and the church is set aflame! And the church begins to smell the scent of victory in the raging battle. Yes, the days are very dark in the West. But God is in the business of shattering the darkness. We must commit ourselves to pray for revival. And we must share the gospel with a new sense of urgency.

Autrey summed it up well when he said, "The entire atmosphere of the church must be permeated with a sense of God's presence. If there is a sense of God's presence, there will also be a revival atmosphere in which the souls of men can be born again."[3] That means changed hearts. And changed hearts will produce a changed society.

The battle rages! "Oh God, revive Your church in this dark hour! Make your people fit for battle" is our prayer.

Notes

Chapter 1: The Battle for the Human Spirit

1. William Gurnall, *The Christian in Complete Armour*, vol.1 (Edinburgh: Banner of Truth Trust, 1988 reprint), 20.

Chapter 2: The Battle for the Human Personality

1. The material in the preceding sections first appeared as "God's Love in the Valley," *Spirit of Revival*, June 1992, pp. 4–6. Published by Life Action Ministries and used by permission.

Chapter 3: The Battle for Society

1. George Barna, *The Frog in the Kettle* (Ventura, Calif.: Regal, 1990), 60–61.
2. Ibid., 115.
3. J. C. Ryle, *Christian Leaders of the 18th Century* (Edinburgh: Banner of Truth Trust, 1885), 104.

Chapter 4: The Soldier's Character

1. William Gurnall, *The Christian in Complete Armour*, vol. 1 (Edinburgh: Banner of Truth Trust, 1988 reprint), 48.
2. J. C. Ryle, *Christian Leaders of the 18th Century* (Edinburgh, Banner of Truth Trust, 1885), 146.
3. Andrew Murray, *Absolute Surrender* (Chicago: Moody, n.d.), 13.
4. John MacLeod, *The Glasgow Herald*, April 28, 1993, 11.

Chapter 5: The Soldier's Family

1. John Wesley, *The Journal of John Wesley* (Chicago: Moody, n.d.), 185.
2. Arnold Dallimore, *George Whitefield,* vol. 2 (Westchester, Ill.: Cornerstone, 1980), 100.
3. Jerry Jenkins, *Loving Your Marriage Enough to Protect It* (Chicago: Moody, 1993), 75, 83, 91, 101, 109, 117.

Chapter 7: The Soldier's Defense

1. William Gurnall, *The Christian in Complete Armour,* vol. 1 (Edinburgh: Banner of Truth Trust, 1988 reprint), 41.

Chapter 8: The Weapons of the Soldier

1. William Gurnall, *The Christian in Complete Armour,* vol. 3 (Edinburgh: Banner of Truth Trust, 1988 reprint), 317.

Chapter 9: The Weapon of Prayer

1. William Gibson, *The Year of Grace* (Belfast: Ambassor, 1989), 252–53.
2. Press release, August 1993, National Network of Youth Ministries, San Diego, Calif.

Chapter 10: Changing People's Hearts

1. Clara E. Murray, ed., *Bunyan's Pilgrim's Progress and Christiana's Progress for Devotional Reading* (Grand Rapids: Baker, 1976), 22–23.

Chapter 12: A Balanced Attack

1. Arnold Dallimore, *Spurgeon* (Chicago: Moody, 1984), 92.
2. C. E. Autrey, *Basic Evangelism* (Grand Rapids, Zondervan, 1961), 30–31.
3. Ibid., 60.

Resource List

A key way to prepare for spiritual battle is to read the Scriptures and books that inform and inspire. The following books will encourage and equip you for the spiritual battles that await. These resources are organized into the four crucial areas that every soldier needs to be ready for battle: our character, our weapons, our strategy, and the nature of the battle.

The Nature of the Battle

Bubeck, Mark. *The Adversary*. Chicago: Moody, 1975.

_____. *Overcoming the Adversary*. Chicago: Moody, 1984.

Gurnall, William. *The Christian in Complete Armour*, vol.1 (Edinburgh: Banner of Truth Trust, 1988 reprint.

Matthews, R. Arthur. *Born for Battle*. 9th ed. Robesonia, Pa.: OMF Books, 1988.

The Character of the Soldier

Murray, Andrew. *Absolute Surrender*. Chicago: Moody, n.d.

_____. *The School of Obedience*. Chicago: Moody, n.d.

Ryle, J. C. *Christian Leaders of the Eighteenth Century*. Carlise, Pa.: Banner of Truth Trust, 1978.

_____. *Holiness*. Phillipsburg, N. J.: Presbyterian & Reformed, 1979.

Taylor, Howard and Mary G. Taylor. *Hudson Taylor's Spiritual Secret.* Chicago: Moody, 1990.

Tippit, Sammy. *Fire in Your Heart.* Chicago: Moody, 1987.

Tozer, A. W. *The Pursuit of God.* Camp Hill, Pa.: Christian Publications, 1972.

The Weapons of the Soldier

Bounds, E. M. *The Weapon of Prayer.* Grand Rapids: Baker, 1987.

Carre, E. G. *Praying Hyde.* South Plainfield, N. J.: Bridge, 1983.

Gurnall, William. *The Christian in Complete Armour,* vols.1–3. (Edinburgh: Banner of Truth Trust, 1988 reprint.

Tippit, Sammy. *The Prayer Factor.* Chicago: Moody, 1988.

The Strategy for Battle

Bright, Bill. *How to Witness in the Spirit.* San Bernardino, Calif.: Campus Crusade for Christ, 1981.

Coleman, Robert. *The Master Plan of Evangelism.* Old Tappan, N. J.: Revell, 1978.

Drummond, Lewis. *The Revived Life.* Nashville: Broadman, 1982.

Thompson, W. Oscar. *Concentric Circles of Concern.* Nashville: Broadman, 1981.